ENQUIRING CHILDREN, CHALLENGING TEACHING

Enriching the primary curriculum: child, teacher, context

Series editor: Janet Moyles

The series highlights some of the major challenges and issues which face teachers on a day-to-day basis in handling their apparently ever widening roles in primary schools. Curriculum experiences can, and should be enriching and stimulating for everyone but there must be a recognition and appreciation of the crucial interface between child, teacher and the context of school and society, rather than a focus on mere curriculum 'delivery'.

Each volume in the series seeks to enrich and extend readers' curriculum thinking beyond the current narrow confines through recognizing and celebrating the very essence of what makes primary teaching demanding but exciting, creative, dynamic and, yes, even enjoyable! The series recognizes that at the heart of teaching lies children and that 'subjects' are merely tools towards enabling an education which develops both understanding and enthusiasm for lifelong learning.

The authors' underpinning, integrated rationale is to enable teachers to analyse their own practices by exploring those of others through cameos of real life events taken from classroom and school contexts. The aim throughout is to help teachers regain their sense of ownership over changes to classroom and curricular practices and to develop an enhanced and enriched understanding of theory through practice.

Current and forthcoming titles:

Florence Beetlestone: *Creative children, imaginative teaching*
Max de Bóo: *Enquiring children, challenging teaching*
Deirdre Cook and Helen Finlayson: *Interactive children, constructive teaching*
Roger Merry: *Successful children, successful teaching*
Janet Moyles: *Playful children, inspired teaching*
Wendy Suschitzky and Joy Chapman: *Valued children, informed teaching*
Jill Williams: *Independent children, sensitive teaching*

ENQUIRING CHILDREN, CHALLENGING TEACHING
Investigating science processes

Max de Bóo

Open University Press
Buckingham • Philadelphia

Open University Press
Celtic Court
22 Ballmoor
Buckingham
MK18 1XW

email: enquiries@openup.co.uk
world wide web: http://www.openup.co.uk
and
325 Chestnut Street
Philadelphia, PA 19106, USA

First published 1999

A catalogue record of this book is available from the British Library

ISBN   0 335 20097 4 (hb)   0 335 20096 6 (pb)

Library of Congress Cataloging-in-Publication Data
De Bóo. Max, 1940–
    Enquiring children, challenging teaching/Max de Bóo.
       p.   cm. – (Enriching the primary curriculum – child, teacher, context)
    Includes bibliographical references (p.) and index.
    ISBN 0–335–20097–4 (hb) – ISBN 0–335–20096–6 (pb)
    1. Science – Study and teaching (Elementary) – Great Britain.
    2. Problem solving – Study and teaching (Elementary) – Great Britain.   3. Curiosity in children.   4. Critical thinking – Study and teaching (Elementary) – Great Britain.   I. Title.   II. Series.
    LB1585.5.G7D4 1998
    372. 3'5044–dc21   98–4043   CIP

Typeset by Graphicraft Limited, Hong Kong
Printed in Great Britain by St Edmundsbury Press Ltd,
Bury St Edmunds, Suffolk

I am deeply grateful to the children, family, friends and colleagues whose enquiring minds have stimulated mine and whose challenges have led to learning and laughter.

Contents

Series editor's preface

Cameo

Glenn has taught across the age range in different primary schools for the last 15 years, specializing in art. In that time, he has had to make many adjustments in his thinking. The emphasis now appears to have shifted significantly from considering the learning needs of children as paramount, to 'delivering' a curriculum over which he feels little ownership and about which he feels even less real enthusiasm! The National Curriculum, with its individual subjects and language of 'teaching', not to mention an impending Office for Standards in Education (Ofsted) inspection, has shaken his confidence somewhat in his own understanding of what primary education is all about. It has also meant that he feels *he* is doing most of the learning, rather than the children – all those detailed plans and topic packs for individual subjects which teachers have been developing within the school seem to Glenn to leave little for children to actually do except explore the occasional artefact and fill in worksheets.

Yet he knows that he enjoys the 'buzz' of teaching, revels in being part of children's progress and achievements, delights in those rare times when he can indulge in art activities with children, is appreciated by parents and colleagues for the quality of his work and, generally, still finds his real heart lies in being an educator and doing something worthwhile. His constant question to himself is 'How can I work with children in ways I feel and *know* are appropriate and yet meet the outside demands made on me?'

Sound familiar? You may well begin to recognize a 'Glenn' within you! He encapsulates the way many teachers are feeling at the present time and the persistent doubts and uncertainties which continually underpin many teachers' work. In the early and middle years of primary schooling in particular, teachers are facing great challenges in conceiving how best to accommodate the learning needs of children in a context of growing pressure, innovation and subject curriculum demand. Yet conscientiousness drives the professional to strive for greater understanding – that little bit more knowledge or skill might just make a big difference to one child, or it might provide improved insights into one aspect of the curriculum.

Glenn, like many teachers, needs time, encouragement and support to reflect on his current practice and to consider in an objective way the changes needed. Rather than trying to add something else to an already overcrowded curriculum, today's teachers should consider those existing aspects which are fundamental to ensuring that children are not only schooled but educated in the broadest possible sense. Only then can we begin to sort out those things which are vital, those things we would like to do, and those things which would benefit from a rethink.

This series aims to offer practitioners food for thought as well as practical and theoretical support in establishing, defining and refining their own understandings and beliefs. It focuses particularly on enriching curriculum experiences for everyone through recognizing and appreciating the crucial interface between the child, the teacher and the context of primary education, including the curriculum context. Each title in the series seeks collectively and individually to enhance teachers' understanding about the theories which underpin, guide and enrich quality practice in a range of broader curriculum aspects, while acknowledging issues such as class size and overload, common across primary schools today.

Each book operates from the basis of exploring teachers' sound – frequently intuitive – experiences and understanding of teaching and learning processes and outcomes which most teachers inevitably possess in good measure and which, like Glenn, they often feel constrained to use. For example, the editor is regularly told by teachers and others in primary schools that they 'know' or 'feel' that play for children is or must be a valuable process, yet they are also aware that this is not often reflected in their planning or curriculum management and that the context of education generally is antithetical to play. What is more, they really do not know what to do about it and find articulating the justification for play practices extremely difficult. Other writers in the series have suggested that this is also the case in their areas of expertise.

All the books in this series seek to enrich and extend teachers' curriculum thinking beyond the level of just 'subjects', into dimensions related to the teaching and learning needs of children and the contextual demands faced by schools. The books cover areas such as creativity, success and competence, exploration and problem solving, information technology across subjects and boundaries, play in the primary curriculum, questioning and teacher–child interactions, values in relation to equality issues, social, moral and spiritual frameworks, and physical aspects of teaching and learning. Each book has had, within its working title, the rationale of the unique triad of child, teacher and context which underpins all primary schooling and education, for example in this particular case, creative children and imaginative teaching. This structure serves to emphasize for authors the inextricable and imperative balance in this triad for effective classroom and curriculum practices. The model we have developed and agreed is shown in Figure 1.

All the writers in the series have been concerned to emphasize the quality, nature and extent of existing classroom practices, and how it is possible to build on these sound pedagogical bases. For this reason, chapters within each title often begin with two or

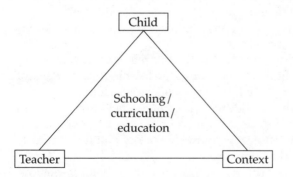

Figure 1 Child, teacher, context

more cameos offering features of practice as starting points for teasing out aspects requiring enquiry, analysis, evaluation and discussion. Chapters then develop their own relevant themes but with consistent reference to what these mean to children and teachers within the general autonomy, and constraints, of the school context.

Issues concerning the *child* take their stance from cognitive psychology (as this book does) and include the child as:

- an active searcher after meaning;
- an individual with particular perceptions of the world and their part in it;
- a person who can reflect on their own learning and understanding;
- a learner with his or her own curriculum needs and interests to be considered;
- an interactive person, learning in collaboration with peers and adults;
- a unique individual but also one with collective needs;
- a member of a 'social' community, i.e. home, family, school, wider community.

Aspects to do with the teaching role lay stress on the *teacher* as a reflective and critical professional who will occasionally but regularly need to stand back from day-to-day practice in order to think about and analyse the triadic relationships and to acknowledge:

- their own learning styles and experiences;
- their own beliefs, values, knowledge and conceptual understanding of pedagogy;
- their need to raise questions about practice and find solutions in an ongoing way;
- their role as mutual learners with children and colleagues;
- their responsibilities as facilitators of learning, as models of learning and as negotiators of meaning with children;
- their role in enabling children's learning rather than always in 'teaching';
- their function as observers and assessors of children's understandings as well as outcomes;
- their obligation clearly to conceptualize the whole curriculum of which the National Curriculum is a part.

When we consider the *context* of pedagogy, this focus subsumes such aspects as the learning environment, school ethos and the actual classroom and school. It also includes such elements as:

- the physical environment – indoors and outdoors;
- the social environment of school and schooling (e.g. is the child an outcome of the context or has the context influenced the child?);
- the psychological environment of school and schooling;
- the philosophical considerations within schools and aspects such as teachers' beliefs and values;
- the curriculum context, including the National Curriculum where this is relevant and appropriate, but also showing where this does not necessarily meet pedagogical needs;
- the frameworks within which the whole concept of schooling takes place and where this fits education in a broader sense.

The overall rationale for each book in the series starts from a belief that teachers should be enabled to analyse their own practices in specific aspects of the broader curriculum as a major aspect of their professionalism. The books are particularly useful at a time of continual curriculum change, when reflection is being focused back upon the child and pedagogy generally as the only perpetuating and consistent elements.

As an integral component, all the books weave teachers' assessment of children's learning and understanding into each particular focus, the intention being to show how the planning>learning>assessment>planning cycle is vital to the quality and success of children's and teachers' learning experiences. With their practical ideas, challenges and direct relevance to classroom practice, these books offer ways of establishing theory as *the* adjunct to practice; they build on teachers' thinking about how they already work in the classroom and help teachers to consider how they may enrich, extend and advance their practices to the mutual benefit of themselves, the children, the curriculum and education in society as a whole.

Enquiring children: challenging teaching sets out to explore curiosity as the basis for learning and teaching, particularly in developing scientific thinking. Max de Bóo expertly guides the reader through a range of exciting and stimulating 'journeys' of discovery into a greater understanding of children's enquiry skills and the teacher's role in challenging children through the contexts provided for enquiry-based learning in an entitlement curriculum. As Max points out in her introduction, enquiry skills and attitudes are generic and transferable and equip children for effective, life-long learning. Like other books in the series, such processes are emphasized as the basis for the most effective education of primary age children.

Covering such aspects as: observing and questioning; planning, predicting and testing; inquisitive thinking; classifying and drawing conclusions; critical, reflective thinking; the search for knowledge; communication and problem solving, Max both outlines and details through a wide range of cameos and exemplars, the concepts and skills which must be fostered, promoted and ensured for primary age children. She emphasizes the need for matching teaching and learning by drawing children's attention to the familiar within an unfamiliar context and vice versa. Teachers are encouraged themselves to be good role models through making it clear to children that they, too, are observers, explorers and tool users and are interested in objects and phenomena. As Max asserts, children need to see that teachers are also searching for ideas and solutions and that there is a significant difference between *drawing* conclusions and *jumping to* conclusions!

In reading this short book, filled with sound knowledge and good professional insight, readers will find themselves challenging primary teaching as it is perceived at present.

The book will delight all those who grow weary of curriculum prescription, for can we honestly say that children in the current curriculum climate have 'the desire to know' or do they have only the desire to complete the task? As Max asserts in Chapter 4, 'enquiry-based learning requires a focus . . . the desire to know something . . . We are equipped to explore . . . to interpret'. How often do we as teachers really require these processes of our primary age children? How often do we teach children to think and to understand their own thinking? Knowing, like teaching, is a dynamic activity and Max de Bóo's intention within this book is to help teachers engage with both and to ensure that children and teachers seek knowledge together and learn to think effectively and efficiently. With great clarity and commitment, the writer reveals how simple, everyday experiences, in the hands of skilled and thinking teachers, can produce a challenging curriculum to meet the highest standards any government could possibly demand.

As a scientist, Max de Bóo's concerns are for children to develop rigorous investigative skills and she shows with absolute clarity how these can so readily be inculcated in young children if teachers work from children's innate and instinctive curiosity. The practical ideas and examples provided by Max throughout the text will be a joy to all readers who really want to engage children in this way and who seek to adopt varied and interesting teaching strategies. Whilst the writer emphasizes the seeing of patterns and the imposing of order as major strategies for children, she has ensured continually that readers develop these for themselves in order better to support young learners.

In Chapter 5, Max asserts that success increases children's ability to face new challenges: the success of this book lies in the quality and range of topics it covers and Max's understanding of children's learning and teachers' needs for support and guidance about appropriate concepts, activities and contexts to provide for effective enquiry-based learning. In Chapter 4, Max writes 'Enthusiasm is contagious'. She's absolutely right! Her own enthusiasm and depth of knowledge will immediately impart itself to the readers of this packed, informative and exciting book and encourage them to respond to enquiring young minds with appropriate – and enthusiastic – challenges.

Janet Moyles

Acknowledgements

My interest in young children's thinking and science led to two years of full-time research working with approximately 70 Reception children, then focusing on groups of eight children in three different schools. I questioned these children in paired interviews in practical contexts based on electricity, food and heat, then worked with these children every week for four to five months: in School 1 (control) as a teaching assistant, in Schools 2 and 3 teaching and questioning to invite descriptions, classifications and explanations, using general scientific contexts (School 2) and using practical contexts of electricity, food and heat (School 3). The children were then interviewed again using the same criteria as earlier. The results showed a much larger increase in responses in Schools 2 and 3 compared with School 1, both descriptions and explanations. Children also volunteered more responses. The numbers are too small for generalizations but the changes were interesting and worth further study.

I wish to thank the following schools in which I was privileged to research children's thinking in science and where some of the children's work originated: Belmont Infants School, Haringey; Belmont Junior School, Haringey; Grasvenor Avenue Infant School, Barnet; Highgate Infants School, Haringey; Queenswell Infant School, Barnet and Nightingale Primary School, Haringey. I wish to thank the following individuals and organizations for their generous permission to use copyright material in this book: John Kitching for the poem 'Why?' and K. Stables, S. Kendall and S. Parker (TERU: Technology Education Research Unit) for use of INSET material (*Key Stage 1 Technology Guidance for INSET Providers*, 1991).

Introduction

Why?
Why are the leaves always green, Dad?
Why are there thorns on a rose?
Why do you want my neck clean, Dad?
Why do hairs grow from your nose?

Why can dogs hear what we can't, Dad?
Why has the engine just stalled?
Why are you rude about Aunt, Dad?
Why are you going all bald?

Why is Mum taller than you, Dad?
Why can't the dog stand the cat?
Why's Grandma got a moustache, Dad?
Why are you growing more fat?

Why don't you answer my questions?
You used to; you don't any more.
Why? Tell me why. Tell my why, Dad?
Do you think I am being a bore?

John Kitching

We are an inquisitive species: we look under stones, we unwrap the present with excitement, we ask questions. We are not the only species endowed with inquisitiveness or curiosity – the dog goes sniffing in the bushes, the chimp peers into the lens of the hand-held camera just as much as the child who searches her grandad's pockets – but human curiosity about ourselves and our universe is boundless.

This book shows how the school and classroom can develop children's enquiry skills and the teacher's role in assisting these. Enquiry skills are life skills and the book outlines reasons for using this approach: having a rationale for a teaching and learning style makes us better advocates of it. The cameos reflect the author's background in primary science but the approach advocated is a universal approach to education.

Shifts in twentieth-century thinking about the teacher's role and children's learning resulted in classroom environments in which children have more opportunities for autonomous learning with the teacher's support. Recent statutory, educational obligations have 'forced teachers to [use] didactive or non-practical, less active methods' of teaching (SCAA 1994: 18). An enquiry-based approach can maximize children's learning while still giving them curricular entitlements.

What is enquiry-based learning? What are the benefits of acquiring enquiry skills?

The term 'enquiry' describes a situation where there is curiosity and a desire to find something out by exploration, investigation and research. Enquiries involve questions being raised, challenges to thinking and problem-solving activities. Enquiries usually require cooperative behaviour and communication with others. Such skills develop *self*-control and confidence in our ability to adapt to a changing environment. Conscious awareness of our skills and attitudes frees them from the original context and affects our view of ourselves and our world, how we react and how we learn.

The enquiring child is an inquisitive learner who has some control in decision making about the strategies and skills used to learn as well as the objectives and outcomes of learning (Menmuir and Adams 1997). Enquiry skills are particularly important in certain areas of the curriculum such as science, but enquiry skills and attitudes are generic, transferable skills and equip children for effective lifelong learning. Enquiry methods can be applied to the acquisition of knowledge and to the ways of acquiring knowledge and positive attitudes towards learning (Johnsey 1986).

The book discusses initiating and pursuing enquiries and the teacher's role in this. Chapter 1 explores the skills of *observing* and *questioning*. Noticing a child's flushed face or a drooping plant on the windowsill enables us to respond appropriately. Asking questions ('Why is the sky blue?') seems to be an inherent human characteristic but can be suppressed in childhood if not given support and stimuli. Successful questioners feel confident rather than foolish – learning to acknowledge our ignorance or lack of skill is the first step to finding an answer, in the Yellow Pages, the hands of an expert, or the library.

Chapter 2 looks at *planning*, *predicting* and *testing* skills. In everyday life we plan everything from a meal to a school visit. We rely on predicting: we could not function without predicting that people will conform to rules and regulations; for example, stopping at red traffic lights. We forget how much testing we used to do as children. In adult life we rely on other people to carry out tests on our behalf (health and hygiene inspectors, quality controllers in toy factories, film censors). Our children need to know about the nature of testing and how criteria are set.

Inquisitive *thinking* is the focus of Chapter 3. Classifying information allows us to process and store information in the memory more easily, without which communication would be impossible. Drawing conclusions helps us make sense of the world by interpreting information ('I feel sick > It must be something I ate'). We seek evidence to avoid jumping to conclusions (a scratching noise in the night = rats). We look to theories or hypotheses when dealing with a frustrated child (fatigue? dyslexia?) or cracks in the ceiling (dry rot? subsidence?). Children need to know how to access available theories, how they are derived, and be able to create new hypotheses if none of the existing theories accounts for the evidence.

Critical, reflective thinking is necessary to the development of mature thinking (Kuhn 1962). Non-scientific theories, such as 'Women are bad drivers', are defended vigorously by people who 'explain away' all evidence to the contrary. Conscious reflective thought gives us access to our ideas and beliefs and allows us to modify these. We need to educate children to have a balanced but sceptical attitude to information flooding in from the media or sales advertisements and to be able to reflect on their own assumptions. This can reduce prejudice and discrimination.

Exploring, investigating and thinking are used in *the search for knowledge*, the subject of Chapter 4. Knowledge is necessary in an interdependent society in which progress depends on the application of increasingly specialized knowledge. No one knows everything – each of us has areas of knowledge and ignorance. Knowledge is not value free, it is set in the framework of a particular society, and each society places emphases on different areas of knowledge: finding your way in the Australian bush or familiarity with the qwerty keyboard.

Communication with others requires language to give substance to our thoughts and voice to our questions and enquiries, explored in Chapter 5. Sometimes words are the only tools we have to convey our understanding of a concept that cannot be seen or touched, such as electricity. Language enables individuals to think and negotiate meaning. People are sometimes accused of using words to confuse rather than communicate: civil servants, scientists, statisticians. However, precise terminology can avoid confusion: good teachers can translate conceptual language into 'child-speak'.

Chapter 6 focuses on *problem solving*, a skill we all need to survive and function well, such as how to get into the house when we have lost the key. Children need classroom opportunities to gain experience and expertise in problem solving: 'The ability of a child to apply her [sic] thinking to the solving of problems will be the key to success in life' (Fisher 1990: 98).

But first, let us start on our own enquiry into the concepts of exploration, observation and questioning.

1
'Look what I've found!': exploring our world

Cameo 1

It is a cold winter's day. Robert and Sanjiv come in after playtime and approach the Year 3 teacher. 'Why is tree bark always green or brown?' they ask.

There is a momentary pause, then the teacher says, 'Only green or brown? Are you sure? Would you like to go back and check?'

The boys put their coats back on and go to inspect the trees. When they return they say, 'It's not – the cherry tree bark has got pink bits and some trees have got grey bits.'

Cameo 2

Year 4 children are absorbed watching seeds and spices in jars of water to see if they float or sink. Suddenly Jack points at the sesame seeds. 'Look!' he says, 'They're all joining together.' They are – slowly and inexorably, the sesame seeds are forming little clumps, then bigger and bigger clumps on the surface of the water.

'You're right!' says the teacher, bending down to see.

'It must be magnetism!' says Jack.

'How can you be sure?' asks the teacher.

Jack thinks. 'I'll get a magnet!' he says. He rushes to the drawer, comes back and dips a magnet into the dry sesame seeds. None of them stick to the magnet. 'It's not magnetism,' he says. 'It must be something else.'

Introduction

The cameos illustrate those occasional encounters when children start an enquiry with a question or unusual object. For example, what preceded Robert and Sanjiv's question? What processes were going on when Jack declared first that it was 'magnetism', then changed his mind saying, 'it must be something else'? What were the teachers' attitudes and responses? And what kind of classroom environment encourages scientific exploration and investigation to take place?

This chapter will:

• describe the nature of exploratory behaviour in classroom enquiries;
• suggest how this can lead to scientific investigation;
• examine why we need to encourage children's exploration.

The importance of teachers' roles as explorers and guides is discussed and suggestions are offered for creating a stimulating classroom environment which gives children implicit messages about expectations and positive attitudes.

Exploratory behaviour and scientific skills

Scientific skills describe the process by which exploration leads to good investigations (see Figure 1.1). Early attempts to define

Scientific skills		Attitudes
Observing Questioning	} *Exploration*	Curiosity Open-mindedness
Planning Predicting Testing (Recording) Concluding/ interpreting Hypothesizing Communication	} *Investigation*	Willingness to tolerate uncertainty; creativity and inventiveness; perseverance; respect for evidence; critical awareness; cooperation.

Figure 1.1 Scientific enquiries: skills and attitudes

national guidelines in England and Wales included exploration as a desirable characteristic in science education. Exploration was later replaced by the term 'experimentation', a retrograde step for primary teachers. Experiments are concerned with proving existing theories, possible with upper juniors but principally relevant to secondary schools and older pupils. Exploration is an essential prerequisite to primary children's scientific investigation, a 'precondition to successful science learning' (Cosgrove and Osborne 1985: 106).

The skills do not always happen in a neat linear way: they are interconnected (see Chapter 2). However nothing can happen without *observation*.

Observing

Observing is *noticing* or *selective attention*. In Cameo 1, Robert and Sanjiv had actually looked at one or two tree trunks. They had noticed something and their observation led to a question. Their observation was probably accurate but limited by the number of trees they had noticed. In Cameo 2, while most children were watching the floating and sinking of peppercorns and cloves, Jack had focused his attention on something completely different – he had noticed the behaviour of the sesame seeds.

Most of us spend much of the time being unobservant. We ignore the sounds on the street where we live or the feel of the chair at our back. We don't notice these things: familiarity and inattention can switch off our senses. Indeed, if we paid attention to everything in our environment, we would suffer from sensory overload. We learn to stop noticing, and children do this from their earliest years. For example, over six years, I tested the observation skills of 6–7-year-old children by asking them how many trees there were between the school gate and the road. Although the children had attended the school for two years no child had ever noticed the number of trees (five).

Readers can test their own observing skills in the following activities:

Activity 1
Can you find the words 'pen', 'liar', 'gin' and 'hero' hidden in the words of the paragraph above? Without a challenge to look for these, there is no reason to notice them.

Figure 1.2　A duck or a rabbit?

Activity 2
Look at Figure 1.2. Now look again. Did you notice the duck on your first glance? The rabbit?

Observing is important – noticing the petrol gauge or a child's puzzled look. Most great discoveries are the result of someone noticing something unusual or observing a pattern, from Archimedes in the bathtub to Lorenz's discovery of 'the butterfly effect' when he noticed a wobble on the computer (Gleich 1988).

Observing is a skill needed across the curriculum: noticing letters in a word or patterns in number or nature. Much of teaching and learning is about drawing attention to the familiar within an unfamiliar context or the converse – for example, a triangle in a spider's web or an upside down image in a shiny spoon.

Observation is arguably the most important of all scientific skills. It is a principal component of exploratory behaviour, a characteristic of good scientific enquiries that lead to investigations. It is also a characteristic of young children's 'play' in which the child is accumulating experience. Play is exploratory learning (Reilly 1974) and is closely linked with the development of intelligence (Sylva and Lunt 1982).

Scientific observation is active, selective noticing. It involves 'deliberate attention' (Vygotsky 1986), which is more than simply glancing at things, or simple awareness of features in the environment. Scientific observation requires focused attention – either spontaneous or directed – seeing the object as an object, or the detail as significant; looking at, looking for, and 'seeing with understanding' (Wenham 1995: 7). This requires prior experience as well as the object immediately in front of us. Scientific observation is a purposeful activity leading to the generation of scientific knowledge and behaviour (Norris 1992; Harlen 1996).

Development

Observation is dependent on the point of view of the observer. Young children's perception develops from egocentric to objective behaviour; from viewing everything as an extension of, or relative to, themselves to seeing the objects as existing independently of the viewer. The ability to show objectivity and deliberate, selective attention has been described by Piaget and Inhelder (1958) as something a child is incapable of before the age of 7. They suggested that young children are capable of perceiving the whole, or the parts, but not both; that is, they 'can't see the wood for the trees'. This has been disputed (Donaldson 1978; Fisher 1990). Where children are given opportunities and stimuli their attention can easily be focused in an objective and attentive way.

Children reveal their developing observational skills in speech and actions. Younger children's comments are likely to include a mixture of subjective or person-centred statements and objective or object-centred statements. Some of the 'comments' will be given in body language. Here are some examples:

Subjective statements	Objective statements
'I like it.'	'It's red.'
'My Mum's got one.'	'It's got black stripes.'
'It's nice.'	'There's four.'
'I'm not allowed.'	'This one is the biggest.'
'It's pretty.'	'It's going down and down.'
(Grimaces in dislike)	(Stretches her arms wide to demonstrate BIG!)

Children's observational drawings reveal their growing ability to notice detail. Five-year-old Emma's drawing of a tree shows she has noticed a big trunk and lots of flowers. Seven-year-old Noel's picture shows close detail of the seeds in an apple. Nine-year-old Andrea's drawing of a glue stick includes the screw thread, the shadows all in the same direction and an attempt at three dimensions (see Figures 1.3, 1.4 and 1.5).

By the time children enter mainstream school, their observations are more likely to be objective than subjective. Research by

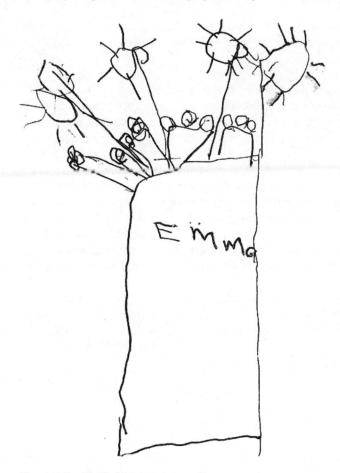

Figure 1.3   Emma's tree

the author, conducted between 1989 and 1991 (de Bóo), showed that, generally speaking, observational responses of 4- and 5-year-old children were, on average, eight times more likely to be objective than subjective. Furthermore, with certain types of intervention, children learned to offer even more objective observations. Where two groups were encouraged to look closely at objects and phenomena over a period of months, these children offered more observations post-intervention than pre-intervention (see Figure 1.6).

Figure 1.4 Noel's apple

Observation cannot be taken for granted and needs constant reinforcement. Exposing children to scientific experiences can develop their ability to 'pay attention' involving their 'intelligence, knowledge and skill in self-regulation' (Wood 1988: 67). Children need challenges too. For example, they usually offer more differences than similarities in their observations (DES 1984) which emphasize the exclusion of objects but are less helpful when trying to see patterns. Where children notice similarities, they are halfway towards classifying objects and phenomena.

As children develop, their observation expands from simple sensory attention to using mathematical tools, sense-enhancing equipment (hand lenses and thermometers) and to making records of observations.

There is a recognizable progression in children's responses indicating their levels of attention, although children will respond in more than one way on different occasions. Figure 1.7 shows the

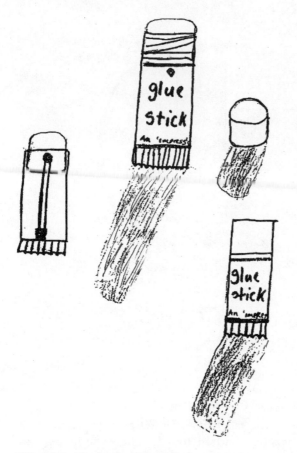

Figure 1.5   Andrea's glue stick

responses given by Year R to Year 4 children when given a mango fruit to observe and asked 'What can you tell me about this?'.

Questioning

Questioning skills help us cope with the complexities of our environment, such as 'Which bus do I need?' and 'Is there a God?' We all ask questions and are dependent on others for answers: such interdependency is the basis of living within a community. Questioning is such a major part of enquiry-based learning that it is addressed both here (children's questions) and in Chapter 5 (teachers' questions).

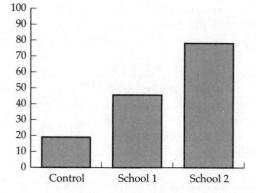

Figure 1.6 Percentage increase in numbers of observations offered by two 'taught' groups, School 1 and School 2, compared with a control group

Responses	Children's comments	
Random	Did you know my budgie died?	P
	I've got new green knickers on!	
Subjective, but focused	I don't want to eat that.	R
	I like it – I had it on holiday.	O
Objective, focused, using senses	It's big and fat.	G
	It's yellow.	
	It reminds me of a potato.	R
	It smells funny.	
	It's soft and smooth.	E
Objective, focused, using measuring equipment	It's one and a bit hand spans.	S
	It's 12 cm long and 7 cm wide.	
	It's got a seed like the orange and the lemon.	S
Objective, focused, using sense-enhancing equipment, more accurate measurement	I can see little marks (with the hand lens).	I
	The circumference is 28.5 cm.	O
	It weighs 316 g.	
	It floats near the top of the water.	N

Subsequent observations involve more sophisticated equipment and measurement, tightly focused on investigations under controlled conditions, e.g. comparison of several fruits, growth, decay, displacement, and so on.

Figure 1.7 Observing

Learning to ask questions is an essential element of a child's education. Children who ask questions are self-motivated and can direct their own learning. Questioning helps us to speculate in unfamiliar situations and solve problems (see Cartwood 1998). It is all too easy to ignore this skill if we assume that young children are always asking questions. Children do ask questions initially, seeking names for things, and then asking 'why' questions. However, in subsequent years, the deterrent experience of classroom environments can leave children reluctant to reveal their 'ignorance' (Tizard and Hughes 1984; de Bóo 1987a).

Children's labelling questions diminish as they acquire a comprehensive vocabulary. This can produce a further decrease in observation and questioning (Johnston 1996). Then there are children's questions which are used simply as tools to attract attention. However, given adequate attention at this stage, children move from asking superficial questions, where they are not interested in the answer, to asking enquiring questions where they wish to clarify something. Children begin to ask clear, detailed questions seeking understanding and information, showing 'mature curiosity' (Harlen 1996: 103). In the right environment, children can be encouraged to take over the ownership of the learning situation by identifying what they wish to know (Symington 1978). For example, Stephen (Year 1) posed the following questions: 'Why do crabs have pincers?'; 'Why do fish have tails?'; 'Why do fish smell?'; 'Why do fish swim?'

Children's questions are not always straightforward. In Cameo 1, the 'why' question asked by the boys sought information but came with an implied assumption that 'all tree bark is green or brown'. Assumptions are always difficult to respond to (Elstgeest 1985) and can close down an enquiry. In Cameo 2, Jack wondered what was happening, but his statement 'Look! They're all joining together' needed interpreting as a question.

Children's questions can appear to be 'silly' or foolish. However, on close inspection children's questions are rarely random and are mostly relevant. If there is a misunderstanding, it is more likely to be our lack of understanding rather than the child's. As such it is our responsibility to seek out the child's meaning rather than impose our own. The more questions that young children ask, and follow up, the more they make sense of themselves and their world (Cortazzi, in press). They become less dependent on being given information, instructions or detailed guidance, and will explore more ideas and phenomena.

In scientific terms, raising questions is the second exploratory skill. There are many types of question but the important questions in science are those which lead to:

- the gaining of knowledge and understanding;
- further exploration and enquiry;
- more specified investigations (Harlen 1996).

In the cameos, the children were encouraged to follow up their observations or questions in the form of a scientific enquiry. This models the way in which we want them to generate their own questions and structure subsequent observations and actions, for example, 'I wonder what's inside?'; 'Which objects will float?' and 'Will electricity go through every metal?'

Children do not usually offer investigative-type questions straight away but with support or 'scaffolding' (Bruner 1968; Vygotsky 1986) children learn to identify what they wish to know and offer ideas and notions that can extend their enquiries and the discussion in the classroom (Gibson 1998). This enhances the learning atmosphere and outcomes for everyone. Once accustomed to the format and techniques of questioning, children take over responsibility for the intellectual search, seeking reasons and understanding. Most significantly, as children begin to formulate questions, they are in the process of formulating answers and are halfway towards predictions as well.

As with the mango (Figure 1.7), we can elicit a range of questions from children which vary from the focused but non-testable to tightly focused investigatory questions (see Figure 1.8).

The teacher's role in encouraging exploration

Encouraging observation

We act as good role models when we make it clear to the children that we too are curious observers; exploring with senses and tools, showing interest in the object or phenomenon. In Cameo 2, the teacher *bent down* to look at the sesame seeds, stressing the importance of careful observation.

Establishing a positive, affirming environment where all observations are valued is one of the best ways to encourage children

Question type	Question	
Wide range, varied, not many testable questions	Where did you buy it? Do we *have* to eat it? What's inside?	P R O
More testable, leading to simple tests/ investigations	Will it taste nice? How heavy is it? Will it have seeds inside like an orange? What colour will it be on the inside?	G R E S
Mostly testable, leading to investigations	Will it taste sweet or sour? Will it have a lot of juice? How many seeds will it have? How many grams will it weigh? Will it float if we put it in water?	S C I O N

Subsequent questions will be very focused and investigative, involving measurement of time, temperature, density and so on: 'How long will it take the mango seed to grow? If we give one seed light and water, one water only and one light only, which one will grow the 'best'?

Figure 1.8 Questioning: 'How many questions can we think of about this mango?'

to voice their ideas. A rich atmosphere of speaking and listening will supply them with adjectives to help them vary descriptions. It can also provide the thinking basis for action (Harlen 1996: 74). Open-ended questions are more productive than closed questions:

- What can you tell me about this?
- Anything else?
- Anyone else?

It is not necessary to suppress a child's subjective responses in order to develop scientific objectivity. Apart from developing language skills to articulate ideas of interest to them, as adults they will make many of their decisions based on feelings and other subjective criteria. It is worth encouraging and valuing *all* observations, from 'I don't like it – yuk!' to 'It's red and yellow and a little bit of blue' (describing a flame).

Encourage deliberate attention. We cannot take children's curiosity for granted. It may have been suppressed in their early years (de Bóo 1987a). In Cameo 1, the teacher asks, 'Are you sure? Would you like to go back and check?' She does not suggest that Robert and Sanjiv are 'wrong' but encourages repeat observations and steers them towards future 'fair testing'.

Purposeful intervention can stimulate observation, thought and action. We can draw children's attention to similarities as well as differences (Johnston 1996) by asking 'What do you notice?' and 'How are they the same?' We can draw attention to fine detail as well as more obvious features of an object or phenomenon (Harlen and Symington 1985).

The more children become accustomed to directing their attention, the more we are teaching them to learn for themselves. We sometimes forget this. Opportunities can be lost in a crowded day, or in misunderstandings about 'unstructured' play where play is seen as somehow not requiring adult intervention. 'Free' play can be imaginative and exploratory, but it can also be limited, repetitive and 'boring' (Johnston 1996). Positive and helpful interventions can occur in everyday activities or in science sessions, in words or actions, focusing attention for a few seconds or longer (see Hayes 1998).

One strategy to encourage observation is to refuse hand contact with the investigation materials (such as musical instruments or coloured acetates) until most children have described something. Clearly, it is necessary for us to know our children before we apply such constraints. Additionally, children who lack confidence or language skills will need support and examples of observations to listen to before they are able to volunteer their own. Children using a second language might be helped by adults or children interpreting their ideas for them. When accustomed to the strategy, most children rise quickly to the challenge so that they can 'get their hands on'! Other ways of engaging attention are shown in Figure 1.9.

There is no guarantee that children will respond to our queries or suggestions. If the intervention is superfluous to their focus of interest they will carry on with their activity, whether or not they acknowledge or disregard our comment. However, frequently, and most especially when we know them well enough to make our comments relevant, children will respond positively to our intervention and compare their observations with ours or follow up our ideas.

Productive questions stimulate observation. A useful mnemonic for this is SAM, which stands for:

Focus of attention	Teacher intervention: actions with and without words
Water tank	Dip fingers in water, hold them up and watch the drips. Repeat, looking closely at the drops. 'Feel' the water in the tank. Smell your fingers.
Fruit	Pick up an apple, trace around it with your finger, smell it, hold it up and look at it from underneath, shake it and listen to it.
Painting table	Feel the end of a clean paintbrush, a lunch box, a child's furry jacket, saying, 'I wonder what this feels like?'
Maths shapes	Hold up a coloured maths shape against a same-colour background. 'Look, it's camouflaged!'
Cars	'Which car is the biggest, do you think? Do the biggest ones go the furthest?'
Living things and lenses	'Can you see how many leaves the little cress seedlings have? I can't count them from here.'

Figure 1.9   Methods of engaging children's attention

SENSES + ACTION + MATHS

and refers to the kind of questions we ask to encourage the full range of possible observations. Examples might be:

Senses:

- What can you see? Hear? Feel? Smell? Taste? (In appropriate and safe contexts.)
- Can you see any colours? Patterns? Are any of them the same? Which ones go together? What makes you say that?

Action:

- What will happen if I drop it? Where's the snail going? What might happen if we push the boat under the water? Burn the fabric?

Maths:

- Which one is the biggest? Heaviest? What shape is it? I wonder if it will fit in that little box?
- What does it remind you of? (> Classification.)

Observing needs time. Time for:

- exploration and investigation (Harlen 1996);
- describing and thinking aloud;
- recording what has been seen.

In Cameo 1 the children needed extra time to go back and check their original observations.

We need to affirm and congratulate children on noticing details, describing or offering alternative descriptions. In Cameo 2, the teacher not only affirmed Jack's skill of observation but signalled that it was acceptable to focus attention away from the floating and sinking. As she said to Jack, 'You're right!'

Encouraging children to raise questions

The classroom has not been the traditional place for *children's* enquiries, but the place where *teachers* ask the questions (Barnes 1976; Cortazzi, in press), seeking from the children information, evidence of learning, confirmation of instructions, identification of offenders and so on. Teachers ask questions and the children try to guess and give the 'right' answers.

For children, asking questions other than for basic information can be daunting. Questions can reveal their ignorance and naivety, their inattention or inexperience, and this leaves children feeling vulnerable. For this reason, the teacher needs to be seen by the children as a questioner, asking questions alongside the children, 'wondering' about the world, showing an open-minded attitude. For example, 'Is the snail holding onto the lid upside down? How does it do that?'

Children need encouragement to 'raise' questions and teachers can often help children to:

- make their questions explicit;
- voice them;
- clarify them;
- share them.

Sometimes the child needs 'scaffolding' (Bruner *et al.* 1966) to articulate their question (see Figure 1.10).

Many of the children's observations can be 'turned' into questions by repeating them with a query (Jelly 1985). For example, 'It's red' becomes 'It's red?' inviting confirmation, elaboration or alternatives. 'This one's the biggest' becomes '*That* one's the

Opportunity	*Intervention*
At the painting table	'I expect you're wondering what colour red and blue make . . . ?'
Designing and making (materials and their properties)	'It looks as if you're wondering if that box will stick better than that yogurt pot . . . ?' 'I know, you're wondering if you let go it will fall down . . . ?'
Puzzled looks	'I think you've got a question in your head but I can't guess what it is . . .'

Figure 1.10 Providing 'scaffolding' to help children articulate their own questions

biggest?' inviting comparison or measurement. In Cameo 2, the teacher turned Jack's statement by asking, 'How can you be sure?' It can take time for a teacher to 'turn' questions or closed statements, which is why the teacher paused in the first cameo, to reflect on ways of challenging the children's assumption in a way that opened up enquiry.

Make time for deliberately inviting questions. On some occasions the pace will be gentle to give adequate time to listen to the less vocal or articulate children. On other occasions children need a quicker pace. At the start of an activity we can show the objects we are going to explore and ask the children for '100 questions' or 'as many questions as we can think of until the sandtimer runs out.' With practice, children scramble over themselves to ask as many questions as they can. We, too, need to think of questions for when it is 'our turn'.

All questions need to be valued for their own sake, whether the answers and problems are resolved or not. We achieve this by showing approval for all questions, realistic or fanciful, original or duplicated. Where a child repeats another child's question, the response is 'Oh, you thought of the same question as Alice did – good for you!' In time, some of the questions will lead to investigations; some will inspire discussion and language development, others will prompt research using books or CD-ROMs. Where the children ask 'why?' questions, turn them back to the children (as with Robert and Sanjiv in Cameo 1) for them to check, predict, explain and seek their own solutions (Elstgeest 1985).

As with observing, we can encourage questioning by refusing hand contact with the stimuli until most children have asked a question. We can also offer examples of our own using the range of SAM questions described on page 18. If the children's questions are restricted to the senses, when it is 'our turn' we can ask questions emphasizing measurement or action.

The questions do not have to be obviously 'sensible' or achievable – question time can be fun, and 'unpredictable' questions can still be scientific! Asking questions such as 'I wonder what would happen if I . . . dropped the raw egg?' or '. . . put the new teddy into the water tank?' will still make the children think in a scientific way about, for example, forces and materials, cause and effect. If it generates laughter as well – good! Learning is allowed to be funny!

Finally, the children's questions are one of the best aids to assessment – they reveal the children's existing ideas at the beginning and end of a science topic or session. Their questions reveal the gaps in their knowledge and understanding: 'Do you know? I saw a great big spider eating flies and it didn't even die! How can spiders do that?'

The classroom context

The atmosphere of the classroom and the school can be conducive to exploration and communicate this effectively to the children and school visitors. It can be difficult turning a second-floor Victorian schoolroom or a temporary classroom into an Aladdin's cave but there are strategies which can stimulate curiosity and interaction.

Stimuli and activities

It is necessary to have something to explore. Children who are raised in an environment which does not stimulate their attention do not acquire the skill of 'attending' (Bruner et al. 1976). The fortunate baby has objects to handle that can be squeezed or that rattle, mobiles to watch and people who talk to them and play with them. Good nurseries and classrooms continue this development by providing stimuli such as construction kits, sandtrays, mathematical shapes, mirrors, magnets and pulleys. Opportunities to explore materials and phenomena are particularly important in a society where children may be spending more time in front of a screen and eating pre-packed foods than playing outside or helping to cook.

The classroom environment needs to encourage children's questions. Tizard and Hughes (1984) found that 4-year-old children asked considerably more questions per day in the home (240) than in the classroom (1). Recent curriculum emphases may have improved the situation somewhat, although some teachers still admit to omitting, deferring or neglecting scientific discussion on the basis that it is 'time-consuming' (SCAA 1994). Questions are easier to encourage when children can observe and discuss real objects and events at first hand (Goldsworthy 1989).

The stimuli need to include familiar and unfamiliar objects. Handling familiar objects reassures children and gives them confidence that they 'know something'. The familiar is likely to include objects and materials that are readily available: potatoes, buttercups, woolly clothes, toys. However, it is always important to introduce the less familiar, the unexpected or unusual: lychees and mangoes, a 'giant' pair of socks, a fossil, an ice balloon, an air plant. These stimulate enquiry, give the children the opportunity to classify and theorize about new objects and allow us to assess their knowledge and understanding.

Unfamiliar objects also encourage children's learning about their own and other cultures, best begun early and positively. Lychees and mangoes are grown in different climates and are eaten by children there and in our own community. The 'unfamiliar' may be familiar to some children in the class and develops their self-esteem as they identify with those materials. One child said, looking at spices, 'That's coriander – my dad uses it in the curry!'

Many resources will be identified by the topic being addressed: musical instruments, hats, plants or torches. Other interesting objects can be collected – for example, bath toys, fans, old (safe) spectacles. Toys inspire enquiry and toyshops are a great source of inventive ideas and illustrate scientific principles: toys that work by mechanical aids or batteries, beach toys or playthings designed to occupy and entertain. My own collection includes a modern version of a Victorian climbing toy, a 'sticky' friction insect (which, if thrown against the wall, staggers down), an ocarina (a small wind instrument) and an electric potato clock. Children's families might provide stimulating resources to challenge thinking and awareness – for example, a track suit or a sari, a Japanese fan or ski mittens. Many questions can be formulated about their design, materials and function.

The kitchen can supply simple resources that inspire questions and further enquiry, such as: tiny bits of dried spaghetti in a transparent glass of soda water; custard powder or cornflour mixed with water to make it both runny *and* 'crackable'; dried peas, lentils or peppercorns, and salt in three little boxes for a 'sound' guessing game. It is worthwhile keeping a supply of these attention-grabbers or 'curios' in the cupboard for filling in odd ten-minute slots, or for rainy days when the children are tired or fractious. Distractions that have a valid learning purpose can calm the atmosphere and help to keep us sane too!

Equipment to aid exploration

We all have extraordinary senses to perceive and respond to our environment. Our hands and limbs are wonderful, accessible aids to measurement and estimation – hand spans, strides and so on. Scientific observation uses these but also needs sense-enhancing tools, mathematical and other equipment. These encourage closer observation and more accurate measurement and exploration of phenomena. Yogurt pots are non-standard but equal units of capacity and the ready availability of a magnet in the classroom means a spontaneous enquiry can be followed up immediately. Aids to observations and questioning (as in SAM) are suggested in the Appendix.

Health and safety

Organizing the classroom for safe practice means setting rules and regulations. Jack was able to go and get a magnet because (a) magnets were available and (b) he knew it was acceptable to get them independently.

Resources for exploration within the school require adequate safe, secure storage space, particularly equipment such as microscopes, electricity kits and CD-ROMs. Many resources for exploration are likely to be cross-curricular and need to be kept in boxes, with lists of contents, plus quantities, on a big clear label outside, copied inside so they can be checked back in. These can be kept alphabetically with usage recorded in a staff logbook.

Figure 1.11 Face by Aaron

Communicating, recording and displays

Not all of the children's responses will be recorded but, increasingly, enquiries require resources for communicating. This can be an exciting part of the process: observations and questions written on pieces of coloured card, on bright sugar paper or a floor book, or on draft paper for word processing. Observations and questions can be illustrated for display or made into a mobile. Questions can be sorted, incorporated into the mounting of a child's work, or turned into a boxed resource for the children to explore when their other work is finished (Feasey and Thompson 1992).

Objects, equipment and media can stimulate representational drawings of children themselves and other objects or phenomena. With or without labels or script, children's drawings reveal their skills and knowledge. Figures 1.11, 1.12 and 1.13 show how

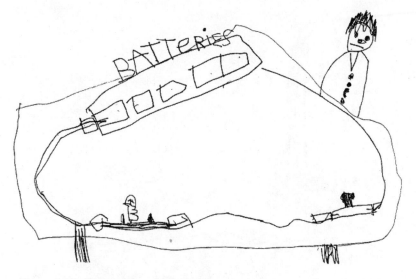

Figure 1.12   Battery circuit by Ben

4-year-old Aaron has knowledge of facial features and skill in locating the drawing on the page; 5-year-old Ben knows that a complete circuit makes the bulb light and that legs are hidden or occluded behind a table; 7-year-old Charlie, looking carefully down into the mirror (position of pupils), knows about perspective and facial features.

The wider context

The prevailing ethos of a school is made clear whenever we walk around it. Teachers and children will be actively engaged in dialogue or practical activities. Independent learners need flexibility to move around, questioning each other, accessing information books in the classroom, school library and computer area. This is movement with a purpose but it can generate a certain degree of noise. However, this is due to enthusiasm and excitement rather than boredom or frustration. The informed school visitor can recognize the difference between on-task noise and off-task noise. It takes experience for someone unfamiliar to school 'noise' to learn how to listen.

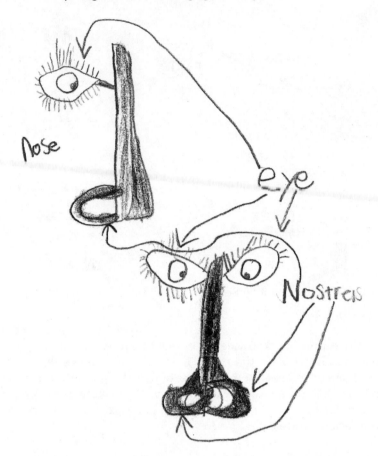

Figure 1.13 Face by Charlie

Exploration goes beyond the classroom and playtimes and dinner breaks are good for exploring outside. Collect a range of playground toys or games to play, introduce these, then use them in rotation to break the routine and challenge fresh thinking. Provide training sessions for playground supervisors so that when children need stimuli or distraction, supervisors can lead a group of them on an exploratory tour of the playground.

Displays around the school can invite interaction and delight school visitors. Children's work can be used to encourage visitors to explore, identify with the wonder felt by the children and begin to see how this stimulates enquiry and learning. Thus a display of children's self-portraits is incomplete without a mirror and questions: 'Some of us have long hair. Some of us have short hair. Is your hair short or long?' Even without an actual display, the outgoing visitor can be challenged to explore with notices near the door stating 'Class 4 knows how many bars there are on the school gate. Do you know? Have a guess and see if you are right.'

The school is part of the life of the community and sometimes at the heart of it. Exploring as an educational goal needs to be communicated to adults who use and support the school. Regular invitations to parents and governors to visit the school on special occasions are, happily, the norm nowadays. These can be extended and expanded to the rest of the community on 'Exploration Days'. Invitations to 'come and explore our school' will raise local neighbourhood awareness, give a focus for children's interactive displays and encourage local school support.

Assessment

1 Do the children show curiosity or ask questions?
2 Do the children offer observations that are person-centred or focused on the object or phenomena?
3 Do the children ask questions relating to the Senses? Actions? Maths?
4 Do the children regularly ask questions that lead to investigations or other enquiries?
5 Are the children recording observations and questions? With support? Independently?

Summary

Exploration is the first step in young children's learning, and has two characteristic skills: observing and questioning. Observation, or selective attention, is fundamental to science and questioning is the way we challenge our ignorance and preconceptions. Teachers can support and encourage exploratory behaviour by adopting positive attitudes to enquiries in the classroom. Children's explorations are initiated and developed when given stimulating resources and challenging intervention.

Questions to ask

1 Observe yourself (through a video or ask another teacher to observe you). Do you offer a good role model in showing interest in objects and phenomena? A sense of wonder or surprise? Do you ask questions?

2 What attitudes do you have towards science and technology? Where did these come from, do you think?

3 What challenging questions or stimulating resources can you think of to enhance exploration, e.g. in the home corner or sandbox? A display table collection, an investigation, design-and-make activities?

4 Observe two or three children. Can you estimate the number of questions you hear them ask in a day?

5 What skills and knowledge do your children's observational drawings reveal?

2

'Do stones float?': investigating our environment

Cameo 1

The Year 2 children are safely on the beach collecting objects to sort into groups for discussion and classification. Darron comes up quietly to his teacher. 'My brother Keith can make stones float,' he says.

The teacher smiles. 'I wonder if they do?' she says. 'Would you like to try that instead of the sorting?' Darron nods.

Over the next half hour he collects an enormous pile of bricks and stones and begins lobbing them into the sea. Periodically, the teacher checks to see how his investigation is proceeding and if he wishes to carry on. Darron is determined. He gradually refines his choice of stone, discards the large bricks and only throws in the smaller stones. Finally, when the teacher comes back, he says, 'They don't. Stones don't float.'

'You're right,' she says, 'but Keith knows how to make them stay up a long time.' She shows him how to make the stones skim the waves and after practising this, Darron goes happily to join the other children. The following day he refuses help in writing up the following: 'I threw stones in the sea and I got some bricks and the stones I threw in the sea they were thin. None floated' (de Bóo 1988b) (see Figure 2.1).

Cameo 2

The Year 4 class are investigating floating and sinking with the student teacher. He has chosen a selection of objects including wood, plastic, metal, stone and fruit for the children to handle and explore first. The children think of questions, tests and factors to control: whether to use cold or warm water, fresh

Figure 2.1 Darron writes up his stone-throwing experience

or salty water, whether the way the objects are put into the water will affect the results. They make joint decisions with the student on the tests. To reduce the emphasis on written work, the student has designed and photocopied a simple record sheet to focus on predictions 'Before' and results 'After' the test.

Georgina predicts that the apple, plastic bottle, wood and paper-clip will float, the stone will be suspended in the water and the Plasticine will sink (see Figure 2.2). After testing, Georgina comments, 'It isn't really fair – the bottle is the only

Predictions

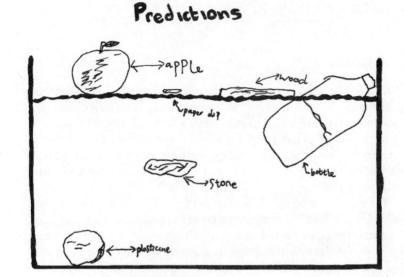

Results

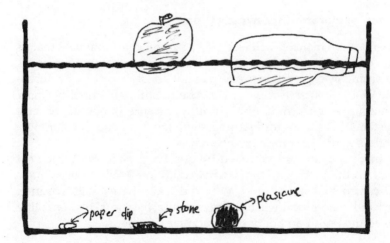

Figure 2.2   Georgina's predictions and results

one with air in it [ignoring the apple]. If the others had air in, maybe they'd float too.'

Introduction

What are the advantages and disadvantages of planned group investigations and individual, spontaneous enquiries? Do the children behave in a systematic way? What validity do their conclusions have? What preparations should the teacher make in advance? What resources and general attitudes make an investigation successful? What is the purpose of the children recording results?

This chapter describes how exploration can lead to investigation and why we need to encourage children's systematic behaviour. Teachers are important in helping children to simplify some of the complex factors involved in investigative science enquiries and recording these. The classroom environment can be structured to support investigation whether inspired by the children's ideas or initiated by teachers.

From exploration to investigation

Exploration by itself will lead an enquiring child into new realms of skill and knowledge but it can be a time-consuming process. Learning by exploration is effective but not always efficient. Teaching is all about making the best use of children's time by maximizing their learning opportunities. Science is one of the best systematic vehicles for learning, evolving from and developing a child's natural exploratory behaviour.

Investigations are preceded by questions, such as: 'Which car will go the furthest? Under what conditions? What do we have to control? Observe?' and 'Why did it do that?' Skills acquired through scientific investigation are transferable skills, enabling us to deal with a variety of unfamiliar situations.

Scientific skills

Figure 1.1 showed how investigative skills are derived from, and linked to, exploratory skills. Representing these skills on the printed page is restricting and suggests that events always happen in a linear way. In practice, the process occurs more like

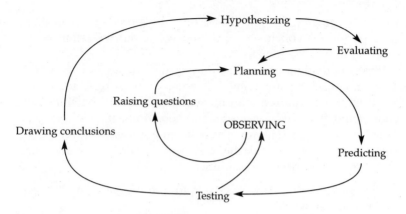

Figure 2.3 The spiral of scientific skills

a three-dimensional spiral in which observing and questioning are recurring, developing features (see Figure 2.3).

A scientific enquiry investigates a question, requires observation before and after testing, and draws conclusions which may provoke even more questions.

Planning skills

Planning skills are life skills: good planning skills make us effective at home and at work and make us more likely to become responsible decision makers. Young children do not use planning skills initially: their behaviour is spontaneous, they think of questions and test them on the spot. We cannot assume that children can plan before they explore, a sequence implied by the National Curriculum for science (DfE/WO 1995). Planning an investigation requires a mental capacity to think through several steps carefully and systematically.

In science, planning investigations is a systematic affair with constraints and controls built in, whether quantities, variables or material limitations. The plan will start with an idea, either selected from the children's questions or chosen by the teacher pursuing the current learning purposes. In Cameo 2, the objects and recording had been chosen by the student teacher, the rest, the questions, controls, resources and safety precautions, had been planned together with the children. In Cameo 1, Darron received little formal support but planned his test on the spot, helped by the teacher turning his initial assertion into a predictive question. He reported his conclusion and later wrote out the result of his investigation.

Most good plans are collaborative, negotiated between children and teachers, referring to necessary resources, tools and equipment. As children mature, acquire more writing skills and understand the need for systematic behaviour, they suggest, or respond to suggestions for, repeat testing or ways of recording their observations. DeLoache and Brown (1987: 110) are clear about young children's capabilities:

1 The young child is an active enquirer, not a passive observer, of his or her world.
2 The child's enquiry is methodical and, to a greater or lesser extent, self-regulated; it is not random or externally determined.
3 The young child's methods of enquiry are in many important ways similar to those of older children and adults.
4 The young child's methods of enquiry are in many important ways different to those of older children and adults.

Young children start from a point where everything must be controlled by others for their safety and welfare. Planning skills develop by taking increasing responsibility for choices and decision making. Children who have good opportunities for decision making at home and at school are advantaged in their functioning. This is one of the tenets of the High Scope philosophy 'Plan, Do, Review' (see Hohmann et al. 1979). At school, the parameters of choice have to be constrained and made clear to the children. The context has to be stimulating and safe.

In an atmosphere of positive expectation and joint research, children can plan science investigations well. When discussing which questions to investigate, they show a high degree of pragmatism. Questions such as 'What would happen if we put it under a steamroller?' are dismissed as unrealistic: 'We ain't got a steamroller' (giggles). 'What would happen if we put it in the oven?' is assessed as realistic and 'What does it look like inside?' receives the response 'We need a hacksaw and a cutting board.' It is rare for children to suggest impossible investigations, unless they are teasing us or are unaccustomed to planning. Even when the children are teasing, the joke can reveal their knowledge!

Progression in planning (and testing) probably develops as shown in Figure 2.4.

Random ideas for tests: a mixture of realistic and fantasy notions, spontaneous or few tests	P R
Realistic ideas: simple tests and equipment; teacher controls all or most variables	O G
Realistic ideas: children identify some 'unfairness', suggest some controls; teacher still controls most variables	R E S
Realistic ideas: more sophisticated equipment, children suggest repeat tests and other controls; some teacher support	S I
Very focused plans for testing: systematic plans and tests, children identify and control variables	O N

Figure 2.4   Progression in planning and testing

Predicting skills

Skill in predicting is vitally important. We have to learn how to use signs and information (people's expressions, the weather forecast) to help us predict and act appropriately. Children need predictive skills in all aspects of their learning: anticipation when reading, estimating in maths, where to draw the head so that the whole body fits onto the page, where and when to reach up to catch the ball and when to take a breath to start singing simultaneously with everyone else.

In science education, there is occasional confusion over the differences between predictions, guesses and hypotheses. The word 'predicting' is used here in the simplest sense – that is, speculating what will happen to an object as a result of a particular action, as in Georgina's prediction in Cameo 2 or the following predictions by Reception children:

Teacher: What will happen if we light the candle?
Davy: It'll melt.
Ann: Go all black.
Alan: It will set the school on fire!
Mary: [Her body droops slowly down to the floor]

Predictive statements contain *two* clauses (spoken or implied), given before the event, suggesting a cause and effect. Teachers often have to infer the cause preceding an effect or use a question to stimulate predictions, as above. Often the language is condensed and implied, as in '*If we light the candle, it will* go all black'. Young children's predictions may incorporate unrealistic or fantasy ideas, such as 'It will set the school on fire' or 'Fireman Sam [fictional character] could put it out.'

Nevertheless, predictions differ from 'wild' guesses which take place in the absence of information. Informed predictions are focused on the object in question, using the speaker's prior experience, even if they do not make full use of the observed details. For example, the question 'Where is Chubut?' is likely to produce an uninformed guess. 'How many words are on this page?' will elicit a more informed estimate on the basis that we have met the printed word on a page before. The prediction becomes scientific if we count the words on a line and the number of lines on the page. (For readers, Chubut is in southern Argentina.)

Predicting differs from hypothesizing which is a generalization. Hypothesizing involves a three clause statement, stated or inferred (see Chapter 3): '*If* we light the candle it will melt *because* of the heat' = 'Heat makes things melt'.

Predictions do not have to be right or even accurate but learning to make them is important in scientific behaviour. Predictions in science have a twofold purpose: focusing children's attention (Cameo 2) and assessing their existing knowledge or gaps in their understanding.

Development

Children's predictions rely on their prior experience and understanding of language, although they can give predictions without speaking, as in Mary's mimed melting. Early predictions do not always show evidence of cause and effect (Piaget and Inhelder 1958). For example, children might respond to the question, 'What do you think is inside the mango?' by replying 'Sort of mango stuff,' or 'We eat these at home.' The first answer offers no new information, the other focuses on personal information. Nevertheless, studies of 4–5-year-old children, such as the author's own research conducted between 1989 and 1995, suggest that random guessing is relatively rare and children's predictions are most likely to be objective (see Figure 2.5).

With support and experience, children's predictions become more objective. Five-year-old Lily reflected on her prediction (see Figure 2.6): 'I'm trying to test which boat's the best with

Subjective / objective predictions
and explanations

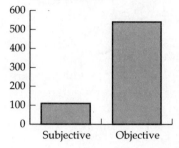

Figure 2.5 Total number of subjective compared with objective predictions and explanations offered by Year R children in the study
Source: de Bóo 1995.

Mohammed. We thought the cardboard was the best but it wasn't. It was the sugar paper' (de Bóo 1993).

In Cameo 2, children used knowledge of the size and weight of objects to make their predictions. Progression in predicting probably develops as in Figure 2.7.

The place of prediction in an investigation is often given after a hypothesis (Harlen 1996) and it is true that, with developing skills, children use their existing theories to give reasonable predictions. However, although children are usually able to give predictions, they need experience and encouragement to offer hypotheses. We can access children's thinking more easily if we ask for predictions in advance of the testing, and choose whether to seek explanations then or after they have reached a conclusion.

Testing

Tests are commonly associated with competition but in reality we are testing things all the time – tasting food as we cook it or the temperature of the bathwater before getting in. Scientific testing is a small well-defined unit of behaviour, an event. It can be a simple act such as bouncing a ball or throwing stones into the sea to see if they float. It can be more sophisticated, such as comparing and measuring the distance travelled by different toy cars after they leave a ramp.

Scientific testing is designed to be impartial and take account of many factors even though some of those factors are out of our

Figure 2.6 Lily's reflection on her prediction

control. Tests involve selecting comparative objects or materials and repeating the tests to allow conclusions to be drawn: children compare their eye colours, observe bulbs for two weeks or jars full of snow for a day.

Question: What will happen if I light the candle?

Guesses	Simple predictions	Systematic predictions
Limited previous experience; limited observation; 'guesses' do not link cause and effect; no new information offered: e.g. 'It'll be alight.'	More experience; use of some observed features and recall to make reasonable (if sometimes inaccurate) predictions: e.g. 'The candle will burn down.'	Previous experience of scientific phenomena; more thorough observation; predictions relate observed features to emerging or known hypotheses: e.g. 'The candle will melt because heat makes things change.'

Figure 2.7 The progression of prediction

Testing is only one part of a whole scientific investigation – it is the collection of evidence. Tests are 'fair' if there are sufficient controls to come to valid or reasonable conclusions. Investigating stones to see if they float is unreliable if we only look at a few stones. Rolling cars down a ramp is not fair if Sally-Ann gives hers a push and Ali simply lets go of his.

Development
Children's initial testing involves sensory exploration and random, repetitive actions. Firsthand experience is the predominant method by which very young children acquire knowledge. Children's testing skills develop with maturation and are dependent on motor skills as well as cognitive understanding. In the early school years, children's testing is still dominated by sensory observations (e.g. watching plants grow on the window-sill or comparing textures in a feely box). However, children can become overconfident and stop observing, making assumptions and jumping to conclusions on limited evidence. Unless these assumptions are constantly challenged with new objects and phenomena, they harden into misconceptions. Cursory glances take over from the thoroughness of earlier, and repeated, testing. In Cameo 1, Darron jumped to a conclusion after observing his brother.

Development is not simply associated with age (de Bóo 1993). Some Reception children, when questioned, know what they want to test and how to make the test 'fair'. Some upper Key Stage 2 children can be unaware of the importance of controlling variables and make one measurement only or change three factors simultaneously – for example, the height of the ramp, the size of the car and the type of car.

Whatever the age, it takes experience, knowledge and understanding to change only one variable at a time. 'Fair testing' is not really *understood* before 6–7 years of age and often much later (Harlen 1996). There is a danger of insisting that children carry out fair tests before this understanding has been achieved. Young children recognize 'unfairness' before 'fairness' ('His piece of cake is bigger than mine!'). Testing also depends on children's knowledge and skill in using instruments: – thermometers and place value, stopwatches and coordination.

Children need to know about testing and how criteria are set if they are to develop a critical attitude to media or other information and evidence. This can be developed by allowing children to practise systematic testing and gradually increasing their involvement in *planning* the tests.

The teacher's role in encouraging investigations

Encouraging planning

Being a good role model in planning investigations usually needs to be implicit when working with young children. Teachers need to be aware of the planning criteria and prompt the decision-making process by reminding the children of organizational details – for example, 'Will you need a cutting board as well?' 'What if other children want to use the sink?'

Nevertheless, even with young children, where teachers control most factors, there is always an element in the planning process where children can take part. If all the details are always controlled by the teacher, the children will not lose their dependency (Harlen 1996). Discussing the criteria together (such as those in Figure 2.8) develops children's awareness of the need for systematic behaviour in their planning. Negotiation improves language and social skills and teachers demonstrate the effectiveness of cooperative behaviour.

What is the question we are going to investigate?
How much time do we need?
Who is going to do what?
What resources are needed? (Is training required?)
Health and safety issues?
Do we want to record observations? How?
Communicating results? How? Display?
Next step?
Evaluation? (Teacher assessment/approval)

Figure 2.8 Criteria for an investigation plan (discussed or written)

Practice and familiarity with the children's abilities makes it easier to know how much to control in advance and how many features of an investigation can be controlled by the children. In Cameo 2, the teacher chose the objects and method of recording but joint decisions were made with the children about the tests and other resources (fresh or salty water etc.). In Cameo 1, where a spontaneous decision had to be made, the teacher considered the time needed, resources (plentiful on that beach), the safety of an unsupervised investigation and the non-participation in a set task (sorting). She approved Darron's plan to test the stones when everyone was doing something else. The message was clear: enquiries are valued.

Training in the use of scientific equipment

Training children to use tools and equipment needs time, opportunities and practice, particularly as these skills have applications in other areas, such as art, design and technology, maths and environmental studies (Raper and Stringer 1987). If training is left until equipment has been identified for a test, the investigation might have to be postponed or children pressurized to learn to use the equipment quickly. Ideas for earlier training are given in Figure 2.9.

Recording the plan and results

Initial planning can be done verbally; later plans will be committed to paper. At the simplest level, teachers will write down children's

Equipment	*Activity*
Stopwatches	Measure how long it takes to go to the cloakroom and return or walk around the playground. Think of an action that takes one minute, or two or three, and try it out.
Thermometers	Measure the temperature of three pots of water from hand-hot to iced water. Mix up some water until it is exactly 25°C.
Hand lenses	Look at tiny seedlings, rough fabrics, woodlice, salt, paper with writing. Find objects that will look sparkly, smooth, and rough.
Microscope	As hand lenses with the addition of cloves and peppercorns, a dead insect, a key.

Figure 2.9 Suggestions for early training in the use of scientific equipment

Version 1

This is what happened (words and/or picture)

Version 2

My question: I want to know . . .	This is what happened (words and/or picture) OR This is what I think will happen

Version 3

My question: I want to know . . . My prediction: I think it will . . .	This is what happened (draw or write)

Version 4

My question: My prediction:	My results (draw, write or graph) My hypothesis: I think it did that because . . .

Figure 2.10 Examples of recording strategies, based on Platten 1993

words for them to copy. Written accounts of what happened might be unstructured, like Darron's (Cameo 1), or simply structured, like Georgina's (Cameo 2). Computer graphing programs can be used to store and interpret data. Angela Platten's (1993) excellent planning ideas can be modified to suit younger children and used flexibly for interest and progression. The recording strategy uses a horizontal A4 sheet folded in half (See Figure 2.10).

Written work should not be elaborated too soon or even carried out for every investigation. Far too often children associate science activities with 'having to write about it'. A simple format for collecting data is sufficient which, together with verbal feedback, helps children to draw conclusions and form hypotheses on the basis of the results (see Chapter 5).

Encouraging predicting

We act as positive role models by offering predictions ourselves and making it clear to the children that we do not always know the answers. We look at the results and demonstrate respect for the evidence. Our attitudes are contagious (Harlen 1996; Johnston 1996) and by showing our own curiosity and open-mindedness, we influence children's perception of science as a theoretical and creative area of enquiry.

A positive atmosphere is one in which all predictions are valued and encouraged, particularly in the early years as children are more ready to risk being 'wrong'. Young children are rarely disappointed when their results differ from their predictions. There is a sense of surprise and entertainment, and further questions usually follow about the behaviour of an ice balloon in water or the extraordinary tastes of American jelly beans.

As well as science enquiries, it is vital to emphasize predicting in all aspects of school life, for example:

- maths: estimating answers to problems;
- reading and listening: the next event in the story;
- music: the theme of the music;
- walking to the hall: will we be the first class there or the third?

In science activities, groups of children can be asked for one prediction each before the start of the investigation in the same way as asking for questions. Volunteered predictions can be followed up with neutral questions such as 'Anything else?' and 'Or?' (de Bóo 1993b). This implies that there is not just one *right* answer.

Sometimes, predictions can be written down for later reference, either by the teacher or the children. It is important to keep a balance between maintaining the momentum of the investigation and recording some of the ideas. Predictions can be written down afterwards as Lily did (see Figure 2.6, page 38) for children to reflect upon.

Children's predictions can be used to assess knowledge and understanding. It is great fun and a privilege to be given an insight into children's thinking. Once, when Year 2 children were given a national, practical set task in science, a 6-year-old boy was asked to predict what would happen to a pebble when it was placed in water. 'It'll float,' he said. The teacher put in the pebble and down it went to the bottom of the tank. The boy's jaw dropped. 'Bloody 'ell, the b****r sank!' he said.

Encouraging testing

We act as good role models when we enjoy the test ourselves and show interest in the results, a willingness to tolerate uncertainty, perseverance and cooperation with others. Even with the strictest of controls, accurate comparisons are out of the question. We are dealing with real objects relevant to the children which make the tests imperfect. We test as systematically as we can but we must acknowledge that the resulting conclusions can only be used to form tentative hypotheses or generalizations as Georgina realized in Cameo 2. We would need access to almost identical objects and sophisticated facilities to make firm scientific hypotheses and even these would be speculative.

Children of different abilities often operate at different levels, some needing very structured tests, while others can work with a good degree of independence. The role of the teacher is gradually to cede control of the investigation process to the children. Figure 2.11 suggests how teachers might do this with a topic on floating and making boats.

Where children's own ideas for tests are followed up, the children have ownership of the enquiries, a greater commitment to them and develop self-esteem. We need to show sensitivity when we challenge children's ideas so that we respect yet do not 'contradict' them. We need to be patient and not supply the children with *the* (= our) answer (Harlen 1996). It may be necessary to monitor the testing to ensure that no extra materials are suddenly incorporated into the test. Reminders about the questions and predictions will refocus the investigation.

Encouraging the development of fair testing needs to be carried out with care. One strategy to use with less experienced children is to illustrate the proposed test (perhaps with different objects) by carrying it out unfairly (e.g. dropping balls from

Reception: need considerable support	Years 1–3: more independent	Years 4–5: independent and responsible
Teacher selects dissimilar objects, e.g. wooden brick, metal keys, plastic toy, lump of modelling clay. Either no recording or drawings with or without labels.	Teacher and children choose 4–6 similar objects of different materials, e.g. plastic, wood, metal, cloth. Teacher chooses method of communicating results and/or method of recording.	Children make choices, decide on which factors to control and choose control method. Materials: roughly equal in sizes and shape, possibly weighed before predictions. Repeat testing. Teacher chooses method of recording and presentation.

Figure 2.11   Joint planning: the gradual reduction of the teacher's role

different heights). Children who are confident investigators will say 'That's not fair!' and our response is 'You're right. How can we make it fair?' If no child objects to the unfair test, they may be unaware of the need for fair tests or lack confidence in making a contribution. Either way, teachers need to ensure that children have only *two* things to compare, that other factors are limited and that children are reminded to repeat observations and measurements before drawing conclusions.

The classroom context for investigating

A classroom and school that encourages enquiry-based learning by investigation signals this most effectively by having resources readily available, even visible, to pursue both spontaneous and planned enquiries. There is likely to be an atmosphere of discussion as few enquiries or investigations can be conducted in silence.

Classroom resources

Children are very realistic about resources and they are helped by knowing, and seeing, what resources are available and permitted. With support, children become adept at identifying appropriate equipment and safety precautions.

Planning and testing

Resources for planning and testing objects in an investigation may be exclusively those materials under enquiry – a collection of shoes to explore or construction kit cars. Increasingly, investigations need tools and equipment: hand lenses to enhance our eyesight, rulers instead of hand spans, balances for accurate weighing. Sophisticated investigations require more advanced equipment: thermometers, digital stopwatches and computer controlled sensors. Children need training in the use of these (see Figure 2.9).

The planning needed for open-ended, negotiated investigations is to identify, as far as possible in advance, what equipment might be necessary for the proposed investigations. For example, an exploration into fabrics produced the following ideas for investigations: burning fabrics (flammability); wearing properties; texture; absorbency/waterproofing; strength. The teacher had to assemble safe burning equipment, containers, hand lenses, microscopes, sandpaper blocks for wearing away, eye droppers and so on.

Some commercial science schemes are helpful in specifying necessary equipment for their activities.

Predicting

Most resources for predicting will be focused on the specific science activity or topic but it is also fun and instructive to emphasize the nature of predictions from time to time. Children can practise predicting and learn that it is 'OK' not to be 'right'. Toy shops supply items that surprise or startle. These and other resources can create a ten-minute focus for predicting and discussing, for example:

1 Stick different-sized lumps of modelling clay inside two separate kitchen roll tubes. Seal these and another empty tube with masking tape. Ask children to predict how they will roll across the floor or table and suggest reasons why.
2 Fill one empty washing-up bottle full of sand, another half full, and leave a third bottle empty. Let children feel the bottle weights. Roll the full and empty bottles down a ramp. Can the children then predict how the half-empty bottle will behave?
3 Use four eggs, two raw and two hard-boiled. Cover a table with newspaper and white sugar paper. Dip the eggs in some runny paint. Can the children predict what pattern the eggs will make when rolled 'gently' across the table? Or not gently?

4 Before the children come in, put a strong circular magnet on the floor or a tabletop. Cover with sugar paper. Use a frame and cotton thread to suspend a small cylinder magnet over the circular magnet with about 2 cm clearance. Ask the children to predict what will happen when you swing the little magnet.

Class rules and expectations: health and safety

Schools and teachers vary in the emphasis they place on developing children's own planning and testing skills – from tightly structured classrooms where children are instructed where to go, what to do and when to do it, to a combination of compulsory activities and greater freedom for self-directed learning.

Opportunities for children's decision-making skills also vary from home to home and from culture to culture. Some children take responsibility in the home very early on in their lives. Sometimes, fears over children's unsupervised play out of doors creates a situation where parents are afraid for their safety and put limitations on their outside play. This effectively reduces opportunities for simple planning and decision making with peers. Science investigations in school can provide this, as long as the parameters of choice are clear and appropriately constrained, and the context is stimulating and safe.

Setting an atmosphere where enquiry is encouraged, both timetabled and spontaneous, means initial establishment of classroom behaviour. Expected behaviour is likely to be universal for all class activities: no running, wear aprons for painting or water, always use cutting boards with craft knives, and so on. Science uses extensive materials and equipment and there will be many rules needing reinforcement. Risk assessment is outlined in school and other policy documents, for example, *Be Safe* (Association for Science Education 1996).

A positive atmosphere sets clear boundaries which do not allow for negotiation: 'I will light the candle'; 'The woodlice go back outside at lunchtime'; 'Throw the paper planes in the corridor, towards the wall'; 'Always wash your hands before and after handling plants'. Clear expectations increase freedom of action within the boundaries.

Teachers who encourage children to plan aspects of their day find that most children behave responsibly. It might seem daunting to give children freedom of choice – there is a risk attached of children's unbridled behaviour that can cause us to fear having 'a riot on our hands'. Nevertheless, self-control is an incremental skill which needs to be taught.

A lovely example of collaborative planning was shown by a Year 2 class investigating fabrics. The teacher told the children that *she* would do the burning over a lit candle using tongs (old pliers) but wanted their help in planning the safety precautions. The children suggested the following, giving their reasons:

- A sandtray + sand ('Sand doesn't burn').
- Do it on the table nearest the classroom door ('So we can run out!').
- A big bucket of water nearby ('Firemen use water').
- A big damp cloth nearby ('My mum put out a fire in a saucepan with a big, damp cloth').
- A bucket of sawdust ('The caretaker puts out things – sick and stuff – with sawdust').
- A jam jar ('Candles go out under a jam jar').
- A fire extinguisher ('We don't want to burn the school down!').

The strategies were all implemented and although the small flame seemed diminutive in comparison with the precautions, safety as well as ownership of the investigation was established.

Opportunist science

Spontaneously motivated learning is often better retained in the long-term memory. Darron's investigation in Cameo 1 was a formative experience for him as he was normally very shy. His self-esteem grew as he realized he could take charge of an individual project with a satisfactory result and adult approval. Current curriculum demands may be such that opportunist science is squeezed out. Teachers can feel dismayed when faced with unexpected enquiries. If set tasks are cancelled, time has to be found on other days to complete the postponed tasks. It is tempting to stick rigidly to schedules but learning objectives can be met if we find the energy and flexibility for *some* spontaneous science: 'Look – it's snowing! Put your coats on, we'll go and feel it, collect it, explore it, investigate it!' Children can weigh, write about and draw snow (maths, english, art).

Figure 2.12   Children investigating dock-side cranes

The wider context

Many investigative enquiries take time. This can mean that equipment and materials are 'in process' along the classroom surfaces and might appear 'untidy' to the uninformed school visitor. The following basic strategies can minimize the clutter or general effect of untidiness:

- *Communication*: label the half-finished models or test materials. Add information as to the purpose of the work.
- *Expectations*: individual/group responsibility – make sure children check, test, record and clear away on a regular basis.
- *Location*: each individual/group has a given place to which they always return their models/materials; equipment is brought out each time and put away safely afterwards.
- *Displays*: make sure the results of the children's investigations are displayed well and changed regularly. Include some of the test materials/equipment as well as the recorded work and questions to stimulate interaction with the children's enquiries. Try to include photographs of the children involved in their investigation (see Figure 2.12).

School resources

Classroom resources need to be supplemented by an adequate supply of good quality school resources. Resources which help investigations are listed in the Appendix. Some resources can be collected from parents and friends, others must be bought – equipment and books – and this has implications for the school budget. Commercial suppliers regularly exhibit at national education conferences and it is easier in such circumstances to compare and evaluate resources for practical enquiries. It is worth using professional development funding for school coordinators (science, maths, geography) and teachers to visit such events.

People

There are many people in school for whom the investigative process may be unfamiliar and daunting. Playground supervisors, teaching assistants and regular parent helpers can all become allies of the process if given opportunities to understand it. They are then likely to use their own awareness and confidence to stimulate children's enquiries inside and outside school on an informal basis.

After-school sessions for parents and governors can give experience of the investigative process and allow exploration of new equipment. Most parents and governors do not get opportunities to explore electricity with new kits, or observe mites, money spiders, muesli or mung bean shoots through microscopes. Yet these people are decision makers and fund-raisers. The purchase of scientific equipment should not *depend* on fund-raising but is often supported, both directly and indirectly, by it. Parents and governors will eventually expect their children to have access to good equipment, and attitudinal change triggers further positive support.

Assessment

1 Do the children help to plan investigations – raise questions, suggest appropriate resources and safety precautions?
2 Do the children make predictions, using prior experience and observations?

3 Do the children suggest ways to make the investigation more 'fair'?
4 Are the children interested and involved throughout the activity?
5 Do the children show confidence when faced with unexpected results?
6 Do the children cooperate with others during the investigation?
7 Are the children able to act independently when necessary?

Summary

Investigations are systematic scientific enquiries. They are derived from exploration when questions are identified that can be followed up by practical tests on objects or phenomena. Testing ideas in a systematic way allows us to arrive at reasonable conclusions. This encourages children to look for, and respect, evidence. With opportunities and encouragement children learn not to 'jump to conclusions'. Helping teachers to plan investigations develops children's self-control and independence. The classroom can become an environment where scientific enquiries are pursued on a scheduled or impromptu basis. Children can be given responsibility for behaving safely, especially when they receive sufficient training in the use of tools and equipment.

Questions to ask

1 Could some of the science enquiries be focused on acquiring a skill?
2 What do you learn about the children's knowledge when you focus on predicting or recording?
3 Practise your own predictive skills: can you estimate how many children will be away from school tomorrow? What does a tea bag look like on the inside? What happens to bicarbonate of soda in vinegar?
4 Can the children help you to plan aspects of the next science investigation such as the resources and/or the safety aspects?
5 Can you encourage the children to carry out simple, achievable, independent investigations?
6 Do the children know the safety code for practical activities?

3

'Babies don't eat real food!': thinking, reason and creativity

Cameo I

Three Year R children are sorting and classifying objects with the teacher: packets of jelly and chocolate pudding, a tin of baked beans, a jar of baby food, a spoon, a big shiny shell and samples of rice, grass and dog biscuits.

Teacher: Do any of these things belong together?
Carl: Yes, these are yummy [chocolate pudding and jelly].
Leila: These go together [baby food and baked beans] 'cos the jars are nearly all the same [cylinders].
Nathan: You could eat your beans out of the shell like a little dish [spoon + beans + shell].
Teacher: Anything else?
Leila: These go in the kitchen [baby food, pudding, beans, rice, spoon].

Further ideas were offered, then later . . .

Teacher: Right. My turn. Can you guess why I'm putting these [rice, beans, baby food, dog biscuits] together?
Leila: Yes, 'cos they're all food!
Carl: Yes, food, food, food, food . . .
Nathan: Not that . . . babies don't eat real food. Or that . . . [dog biscuits].
Carl and Leila: Yes . . . food for dogs!
Teacher: What about the grass then?

Figure 3.1 Sasha's fairground game

Cameo 2
A Year I child is given a worksheet to practise and reinforce skills in addition. The worksheet shows a fairground game 'Roll 2 balls and make a score'. Numbers are written above the box holes and two balls have been drawn in, implying that the sum is $1 + 4 = 5$. Sasha draws in what she declares are the 'missing' balls and explains why she has written down: $2 + 2 = 4$ (that is, two white balls + two black balls = four balls altogether) (see Figure 3.1).

Cameo 3
One Monday morning, Year 3 children inspect their plants on the classroom window-sill. Out of 32 plants, one plant is found to be infested with blackfly. Sean takes it to show the teacher in dismay. They discuss the dreadful result and then Sean writes the following: 'My indoor plant is dying because the leaves are all crunchy. Little black things are eating them.' He is proud of his writing (see Figure 3.2) but still distressed. 'Why mine?' he asks.
'Why do you think?' asks the teacher.
Sean thinks, then smiles. 'Mine must be the tastiest!'

Cameo 4
A 5-year-old child is being interviewed on the subject of heat, using pictures and objects as stimuli.

Teacher: What will happen if we put this [pan of milk] on the cooker?
Noam: It will go all bubbly.
Teacher: Why will it go all bubbly?
Noam: Because the hot of the cooker . . .
Teacher: But how does the hotness get into the milk?
Noam: It goes all over bottom and it makes a little gap and it squeezes through the hole and gets into the milk.
Teacher: So the heat makes a little hole in the saucepan?

Figure 3.2 Sean's indoor plant

> *Noam:* You can't see it, it's too really . . . sort of . . . [indicates sliding around with his hands].
> *Teacher:* Anything else?
> *Noam:* [thinks] No. Oh, if it had holes the milk would fall through [shrugs].

Introduction

What thought processes are occurring here? How should we respond to the variety of ways in which children sort and classify? What is the difference between *drawing* conclusions and *jumping* to conclusions? What particular language skills are needed before children can hypothesize? What questions did the teachers ask and why? What resources were used to support these children in their thinking?

This chapter looks at young children's thinking and their ability to reason and hypothesize. 'Thinking' requires a particular emphasis as many classroom activities are prescriptive and do not encourage children to 'think for themselves'. Thinking is too important a skill to be left to chance; supportive strategies and teaching help children to think and function more effectively.

Objective thinking

The first step in helping children to think for themselves is teaching them to be objective. Objective thinking allows us to abstract ideas and processes from their initial context and apply them in other situations. 'Red-ness' not only describes a red ball but also a hat, a bus or a postbox. Objective thinking allows us to have several alternative perspectives on an object or phenomenon and this assists our reasoning and choices of action. Subjective or egocentric thinking is constricting and takes no account of all the factors influencing the outcome. Objective thinking is organizational (classification), rational (drawing conclusions), problem-solving, creative (hypothetical) and reflective. Shared communication and identification with others depends to a great degree on objectivity in that it allows us to share our perspectives.

Our thinking can never be wholly objective or value-free – it is the outcome of our individual experience in a particular cultural and social context. We need to accept this and respond accordingly, viewing opinions, 'scientific facts' and media reports with open-minded scepticism. We also need to evaluate our own thinking and subjectivity.

Development

Under appropriate guidance, children's thinking develops from initial subjective responses to objective reasoning and from there to metacognitive or critical, reflective thinking. There is a hierarchy of developmental behaviour but also a cumulative effect as children continue to use subjective responses long after they have acquired objectivity. With experience, children are increasingly able to choose which response to give and identify when subjective responses are inappropriate. Metacognitive thinking is objective awareness of our own thinking and usually develops later, but this thinking can be encouraged if children are given opportunities and stimuli (Fisher 1990). The cameos at the beginning

Metacognitive thinking

Critical, reflective, thinking about ideas (e.g. Noam, Cameo 4)

Objective thinking

Object-centred (e.g. foods, Cameo 1)

Subjective thinking

Person-centred (e.g. 'Yummy', Cameo 1)

Figure 3.3   The development of thinking

of this chapter were chosen to show the range of different types of children's thinking. Development probably looks like the model shown in Figure 3.3.

Effective education is geared towards teaching children to think objectively although we must ensure that children always have opportunities to express personal responses. This applies to scientific activities as much as to other areas of the curriculum. Emotional and intellectual development are interdependent (Piaget 1978b).

Classification

An important step in children's thinking is classification; seeing patterns and imposing an order on the world (Bruner 1968). Without classification we would have to experience each object and describe each detail to define the object or events that we speak of, and memorize vast quantities of information for retrieval. This represents an incredible cognitive overload.

Classification is used here in the active sense – that is, a method for sorting objects and phenomena by similarity of characteristics or other criteria. Sorting and classifying is a thinking bridge between description (observed characteristics) and generalizations (hypotheses), an act of inductive thought which unites several individual characteristics into a whole.

Objects can be classified subjectively (using personal, unpredictable or thematic criteria) (Markman and Hutchinson 1984) or

Subjective

Things I like/don't like (personal)
In the kitchen (thematic)
You can eat beans out of a shell (dish) (functional)

Objective

Colour (brown/white) (Abstract idea or concept of colour)
Food/not food (More generalized concepts: humans; edible/non-edible)

Figure 3.4 Subjective and objective classification

objectively (using systematic criteria). Both ways are used by the children in Cameo 1 (see Figure 3.4).

Objective or scientific classification involves sorting in a hierarchy of groups, such as: Cox's and Bramleys = apples; apples and pears and bananas = fruit; fruit and cereals and meat = food; and so on. Depending on the purpose of the classification, objects and phenomena can be included in a great variety of classes. Try it. Readers could, at one and the same time, belong to any or all of the following classes:

Animals	Non-smokers
Employees	Car owners
Teachers	Arachnophobes
Humans	Europeans
Taxpayers	Skiers

Development

As very young children begin to perceive objects and acquire language, they learn to give labels to objects ('Dada'). This behaviour is itself an act of classifying (Vygotsky 1986) – 'Dada' implies 'not-Dada'. The label 'chair' excludes something that is 'not-chair' and children quickly include armchairs, high chairs, dining chairs as 'chairs' and tables, balls and teddies as 'not-chairs'. The naming of these and the growing awareness of their properties gives children the ability to identify and classify.

Children's ability to classify will develop; from:

- knowledge gained from prior experience of the objects (often still subjective) and their properties ('mine', 'yummy');
- the ability to abstract the property or characteristic from the object (brown, cylinders);
- more sophisticated vocabulary and meaning associated with those objects and their properties (foods > edible/inedible/toxic);

to:

- a conscious, conceptual understanding of similarity and difference.

The importance of classification has implications for the classroom where children are most often presented with objects to classify by mathematical criteria or other single attributes (size, shape, colour). While this makes assessment easier, it reduces children's opportunities to make broader generalizations and show their thinking skills and ingenuity.

Reasoning: drawing conclusions and logical thinking

In everyday situations we are putting 'two and two together' before we act – for example, 'The children in the corner are unusually quiet > Are they are plotting something?' Logical thinking is a useful step by step approach to an enquiry, investigation or problem and helps us eliminate poor solutions to those problems. Reasoning involves drawing conclusions and inferences. Thinking like this always goes *beyond* the tangible and uses our collective experience, recalled and cross-referenced with the new experience. It involves an act of the mind, a reflection on what is known, usually without us being aware of the process – for example, Sasha's inference in Cameo 2. Piaget (1974) argued that logical reasoning is a central factor in intelligence and that science is the application of that skill when investigating the physical world.

The term 'drawing conclusions' describes a result or a statement which draws together a cause and effect as we try to make sense of our experience or observation. In speech, we often hear half of the cause and effect statement and infer the other half: (When I blew on the candle . . .) 'That made the flame wobble!' If we ask children to interpret the graph in Figure 3.5, we expect them to conclude 'Most of us have got brown eyes.'

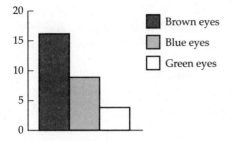

Figure 3.5 Colour of class 2's eyes

Drawing conclusions differs from 'jumping to conclusions' in that we look at and control or compare more than one feature. Children with less experience often base their conclusions on limited evidence which is why we need to encourage them to double check and, increasingly, control some of the variables.

Development

The young child is bombarded with information and uses strategies to process the information more effectively (Bruner 1968). Reasoning in the early years is normally inductive – that is, arguing from a specific piece of information to a generalization. It allows children to classify, reason and hypothesize, as with Sean in Cameo 3: 'Plants die [if] little black things eat the leaves'.

Inductive thinking will not necessarily give us the best *possible* answer but the best *available* answer. It is a method of providing us with 'the best fit' at the time.

It can be difficult to recognize children's developing skills in reasoning, particularly as the evidence is often sandwiched between examples of 'faulty' reasoning. Children may:

- reverse cause and effect;
- ignore some results altogether;
- import new, personal information or animism into their conclusions.

This happens quite often with children between 4 and 6 years of age: 'You mustn't touch the electric wires [television cable] 'cos our telly's right next to the wall, so I can't.' Where we have uninterrupted time with a child, we can sometimes unpick the child's thinking as in the case of Sasha (Cameo 2) and assess the degree of knowledge and reasoning.

Reasoning in highly abstract contexts is not typical of young children's thinking, but in the presence of real objects and situations it is clear that children can reason well and make inferences (Donaldson 1978).

Hypothetical or creative, intuitive thinking

Hypothetical thinking is intuitive thinking, a leap of understanding (Popper 1988). Hypothetical thinking uses prior knowledge but makes new connections and creates original ideas (Bruner 1971; McPeck 1981). In Cameos 3 and 4, Sean and Noam created unique theories using their previous knowledge and the immediate stimuli – they 'invented their own wheel' or constructed their own explanations. Older children's hypotheses begin to make use of several observed features as well as theoretical knowledge (see Chapter 2, Cameo 2).

Hypotheses do not have to be *true* but they do need a recognizably rational structure. They are based on the correct use of connective words (Donaldson 1978) such as 'if, when, then, because'. For example: 'If we put the pan on the cooker [then] it will get hot because heat can go through/into a saucepan.' In some cases the hypotheses are testable, either practically (testing with a magnet in Chapter 1, Cameo 2) or by mental modelling (Cameo 4, this chapter: Noam and the saucepan + holes).

Children who are limited in the language of the discussion are disadvantaged in showing their skills in hypothesizing. While it is possible to use body language to illustrate a prediction or a conclusion, it requires spoken language ('because') to offer an explanation or a generalization. Using the word 'because' does not guarantee understanding – young children will use it long before they understand the concept of cause and effect (Chomsky 1980). For example, children use the word 'because' in place of 'and' or 'but': 'Sweets aren't good for our teeth 'cos I can have one every day.'

Development

Children's initial hypotheses are inductive, based on single ideas. Later, children begin to have some general principles or hypotheses in place and use these to think deductively. Deductive thinking allows us to use previous theories to make realistic predictions and act with a degree of confidence in the outcome. For example: The light goes out. We think: 'Electrical equipment sometimes breaks down.' The cause could be: a bulb defect, a fuse or power cut. We would then test each theory.

Without such theories, children's early hypotheses may be unrealistic, or 'illogical' (to adults). A simplified progression of creative hypothesizing is shown in Figure 3.6.

Children can offer objective conclusions and hypotheses if encouraged. In a study of Year R children over 6 months, most children gave objective rather than subjective explanations. Figure 3.7 shows the relative change in the numbers of objective conclusions and hypotheses offered – children in School 1 and School 2 were given additional opportunities, stimuli and questions to encourage thinking skills. The control group was not.

Young children's ability to hypothesize will depend on factors such as:

- the extent of their first-hand experiences (Kuhn 1962; Fisher 1990);
- their confidence in the language of discussion;
- the attitudes and support of the people around them;
- the stimuli of the moment.

Children have explanatory mechanisms in place (Carey 1985) and, if they are offered interesting phenomena and are confident and relaxed, they will create plausible and rational hypotheses. Additional support or 'scaffolding' (Bruner 1966) helps children to perform beyond their existing performance levels (see Merry 1998).

Sometimes children's invented theories share similarities with theories through the ages. However amusing or irrational it seems, Noam (Cameo 4) created a theory of heat transfer which resembles seventeenth- and eighteenth-century ideas of heat as a 'fluid' that can flow in and out of materials. Perhaps every scientific discovery contains an irrational element or creative intuition (Popper 1988) and this makes hypothesizing or the development of the intuitive faculty very important (Fisher 1990).

There are dangers of leaving children with misconceptions or letting intuitive thinking stand on its own, particularly where

Very limited experience of phenomena	Limited but stimulating experience of phenomena	More experience of varied phenomena	Experience of phenomena and of hypotheses	Considerable experience of many hypotheses
Infant child (0–3 years): no hypotheses	Young child (preschool): few original hypotheses	Older child (5–8 years): several original hypotheses	KS2/Secondary pupil: fewer original hypotheses	Adult/Scientist: very few original hypotheses

Figure 3.6 The progression of creative hypothesizing

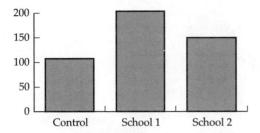

Figure 3.7   Percentage increase in objective conclusions and hypotheses

'everyday theories' persist in spite of conflicting evidence (Baron 1985; CLIS 1987). Misunderstandings and prejudices can result from actions based on false hypotheses, even scientific hypotheses. There are disadvantages too for open-minded young theorists, for it is likely that many of their theories will be proved 'wrong' and it is easy to lose confidence (Bruner 1971).

The advantages of intuitive or hypothetical thinking are that young children can suggest hypotheses without having to account for the complexity of the factors involved. Furthermore, positive attitudes are encouraged. There can be a sense of delight and satisfaction when a 'satisfactory' (explaining some of the features) hypothesis has been generated and the whole picture emerges. Sayings illustrating this feeling are numerous: 'The penny's dropped!'; 'It's clicked!' Seven-year-old Tom's leap of understanding about symmetry gave him a real sense of delight (see Figure 3.8): 'When you put a mirror on a leaf it goes symmetrical. That means it's whole. It is a bit like magic.'

In some situations, children are expected to write up their science work by *putting the right answer* even if the experiment appears to lead to different conclusions. The formalism of school learning, particularly in maths and science, has devalued intuition (Bruner 1971) and creative thinking is discouraged by this. Science is seen as a body of facts rather than a process of theorizing and testing various sets of beliefs.

As products of personal and cultural influences, our thinking is set in an individual frame of reference and will always show aspects of subjectivity. That is why mature thinking would be incomplete without the element of critical, reflective thinking or metacognition.

Figure 3.8 The magic of discovery

Critical, reflective thinking or metacognition

Teaching and learning: a play in four (or more) acts (de Bóo 1996):

Act 1: 'You don't know.'
'Don't I?'
Act 2: 'You don't know.'
'I know I don't.'
Act 3: 'You know.'
'Do I?'
Act 4: 'You know.'
'I know I do.'

Critical or reflective thinking is concerned with our ability to assess the effectiveness of our *thinking* rather than the ability to evaluate our methods of investigating or conclusions. The latter is more involved in problem solving (see Chapter 6). Reflective thinking can exert a controlling influence over the thinking process itself (Norris 1992). A computer can receive incoming data, process it, and respond. However, a computer does not *know* that it can think, it cannot think about the process of thinking, or change the way it responds unless it has been programmed to do so. In contrast, human beings are conscious of the *process* of thinking. In Cameo 4, Noam reflected on his own theorizing, recognized a flaw and rejected the theory.

Thinking critically is not easy: our cherished theories can be proved 'wrong' and this can damage our self-esteem or require readjustments in our behaviour – an uncomfortable process. However, critical thinking reduces prejudice and contributes to 'a more rational and humane society' (McPeck 1981: vi).

Scientific theories are always provisional (Hawking 1988; Popper 1988) and subject to criticism and change, such as:

The Earth is flat.
No, it's not. It's a sphere.
No, it's not. It's a spheroid.
No, it's not. It's a . . . ?

Revising theories always needs the application of critical, reflective thinking.

Development

Reflective or critical thinking is unlikely to occur spontaneously during the primary school years (Piaget and Inhelder 1958; Kuhn 1962) although research into teaching children to think (Fisher 1990) suggests that, with training, young children can use such metacognitive processes. They have 'the capacity to reflect on [their] own acts' (Bruner and Haste 1987: 91), like the children in Cameo 1 (food for dogs), 'self-monitoring and self-correcting' (p. 91). Critical thinking 'can be taught successfully as a skill' (p. 91), and in particular, hypothetical thinking leads to critical thinking. Awareness of ideas *as* ideas stimulates the beginnings of critical thinking (Baron 1985; Norris 1992).

Children's ability to think critically is dependent on:

• experience;
• the development of self-control and self-awareness;

- linguistic and reading abilities (Donaldson 1978);
- subject knowledge (McPeck 1981; Fisher 1990).

The teacher's role

Encouraging classification

Children need a wide range of opportunities to practise and develop sorting and classifying skills. Initially, children will try to 'read our minds' to find out what they think we *want* them to say. Learning that any and all criteria are valued requires a positive atmosphere. We need to affirm the children's ideas for inclusion or exclusion and seek clarification if needed. For example, 'I think I know why you've chosen those but can you tell me just in case?' We can reinforce the idea of acceptable alternatives by giving other children opportunities to classify the objects in different ways, as in Cameo 1.

Children often put two items together only. We can encourage larger groupings by offering another object with the same criterion for the child to include or exclude.

We may have a category in mind which children have not used. When it is 'our turn' we can select those items which reflect the concept, such as 'living/never alive', 'electric/not-electric' or 'food/not-food' (Cameo 1). If children cannot guess our criteria, they may lack understanding of those concepts.

More opportunities can be provided for children to sort and classify with, for example, exploratory tabletop activities using boxes, paper plates or hoops into which objects can be sorted, as a five-minute exercise at class discussion time. Questions can be added, such as 'How many ways can we sort these objects?'

We can vary the criteria with objects that are focused, inspirational or surprising (see the discussion on classroom context in the next section). We might limit the number of objects for less experienced children and keep two or three extra objects to change and renew the set as well as challenge children's criteria. Experienced children can be given specific conceptual criteria to supply written or real objects: reflectors, electrical devices, pliable materials. It is important to keep options open for children to choose by subjective criteria ('I like it') and objective criteria (colour, pattern, shape), by functional as well as thematic groupings ('belongs in the kitchen'). Confidence and ability in classifying leads to the skill of hypothesizing.

Encouraging children to draw conclusions

Children tend to assume that teachers 'know everything'. This can be a disadvantage. In scientific enquiries it is not only easier but necessary to play down this assumption. Children need to see that teachers, too, are searching for ideas and solutions. Acknowledging ignorance is one way of doing this; referring to other people's expertise or reference books is another.

Enthusiasm is contagious. Showing an obvious interest in the outcomes of a test, investigation or event is one of the best ways to encourage children to draw conclusions, such as: 'Did you see what happened!' Positive atmospheres are also those in which children draw surprising or unrealistic conclusions and yet these are accepted by the teacher. In response to children's unexpected or 'erroneous' conclusions we can say, 'Well, it certainly looks like that, doesn't it?' If appropriate, we can follow this with 'Is there any way we can check this?' (child suggests re-testing), or 'I wonder if it would do that again?' (adult suggests re-testing).

An effective atmosphere for supporting reasoning skills is one in which most of the tangle of multiple variables have been streamlined (or controlled) in advance, by the teacher and the children. This allows children to come to straightforward conclusions. Sean's plant (Cameo 3) had been exposed to the same conditions as everyone else's. His conclusion was clear and justifiable.

Enquiries in the primary classroom are imperfect – we work with unsophisticated materials and equipment which means that our conclusions will not always exemplify accepted theories. Being scientific means repeating practical tests so that conclusions can be confirmed, modified or reversed.

Questioning encourages children to articulate their thinking. Questions can fall into three categories: asking the children for their conclusions (the effects); inviting them to recall the original action (the causes) and their predictions; and inviting them to suggest further tests or applications of their conclusions. For example:

1 *Conclusions/effects:* 'What has happened?' 'Did you hear that?' 'What do you notice now?'

2 *Recall/causes:* 'What did you do to make it go slower?' 'What made it do that?' 'Do you remember what we thought it was going to do?'
3 *Next step/application:* 'What are you going to do next?' 'Can you make it go even slower?' 'So when you put it in the sun it melted? Where should we put it if we don't want it to melt?'

Establishing the cause and effect provides the opportunity for teachers to ask 'Why do you think it did that?' and acts as a springboard for children to think of their own hypotheses. Young children's emerging hypotheses are often like supplementary conclusions, as in the example below. In this case, David was speculating from his observations and previous knowledge of balloons and air and sound – he could not *see* any air.

Teacher: [holding a balloon for a child to burst] Did you hear anything then?
David: It went Ssss! [effect]
Teacher: What did you do to make it go Ssss?
David: [laughs] I stuck a pin in it! [cause]
Teacher: Do you think it will go Ssss if you stick another pin in it? [invites further testing]
David: It might do . . . [tries]. No, it's all finished.
Teacher: I wonder what made it do that? [invites hypothesis]
David: I think all the air came out. [emerging hypothesis/ conclusion]

Using and interpreting recorded work
One of the chief reasons for recording work is to help children to draw reasonable conclusions. This not only refers to tables and graphs but any record of work: a drawing or illustration, a piece of writing or a model.

The conclusions may appear to be basic to adults. However, adults can take a great deal for granted, such as in Sasha's case (Cameo 2). She noticed the empty spaces, inferred that empty spaces required balls in them, and gave the 'wrong' answer. The author of the book had assumed experience of a fairground game.

Displayed work or events can be used for daily practice in interpreting: 'Can anyone remind us how many children have black hair?'; 'Which bean is the tallest so far?'; 'Has anybody seen where the shadow has moved to yet?'

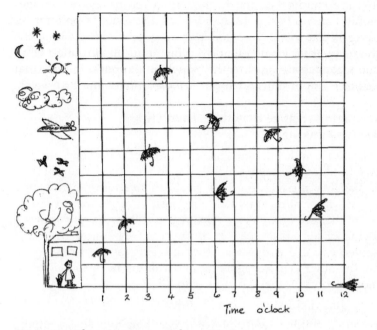

Figure 3.9   The adventures of the red balloon

Spontaneous enquiries
It is important, whenever possible, to make use of unusual or spontaneous events to record and interpret real or imaginary conclusions. On one occasion in the playground, my red umbrella blew out of my hands. We all scampered after it but the wind snatched it up and blew it out of reach. Again and again the children chased it before we caught it. Back in the classroom, I gave squared paper to my Year 2 class to make a graph. They were in a transition stage of graphing and had limited understanding of metric height. We made the x axis simple with 'times o'clock'. The y axis used negotiated icons for height: me, a house, a tree, birds flying, then aeroplanes, and so on (see Figure 3.9). Children made graphs of the adventures of *their* red umbrellas so that it was possible to encourage individual interpretation: 'Where was *your* umbrella at seven o'clock?'; 'What time was it when your umbrella flew up to the clouds?' (Any event or story offers similar inspiration.)

Inviting children to clarify their own recordings encourages reasoning and is best done in a verbal discussion soon after recording. Where this is not possible, it is a good idea to continue the dialogue on their written work. Adding a question to their work triggers conversation when the opportunity arises, implies that dialogue is important, and shows we value them and their work.

Encouraging creative hypotheses and critical, reflective thinking

Our attitudes and comments have an important influence on children's thinking. By saying aloud, 'I wonder why the bumble-bee bangs against the window?' we establish an environment where enquiry is fascinating to us all. Being positive might mean keeping quiet in the face of an 'error'. Six-year-old Lucy's work shows a drawing of herself as seen in the mirror (see Figure 3.10). She observed one eye with a tear duct and generalized from this to draw the other eye. Recognizing and valuing her generalization is more important that asking her to 'do it again'.

Frequency of opportunity
Very often, children will not volunteer their hypotheses unless invited to do so. If children are not accustomed to being asked for their opinion at home or at school, they will be surprised by our interest. Older children can be wary of giving the 'wrong' answers. The key question to elicit children's hypotheses is an open-ended one of: 'Why do you think that?' In Cameo 3, Sean's response to this question gave a hypothesis that used the evidence, a valid conclusion and recalled knowledge.

Children may not answer immediately, in which case they need time and more opportunities to respond within practical contexts. All explanations should be accepted, whether unrealistic or justifiable, or whether 'because' is used meaningfully or inappropriately. Practice will improve children's skills and self-confidence.

It also helps if other children are invited to interpret the same phenomenon or results by asking questions such as: 'Could it be anything else?' or 'anyone else?' or repeating their statements with a query, as in Cameo 4: 'So the heat makes a little hole in the saucepan?' The restating of the child's comment in a positive tone of voice not only confirms that the teacher has heard the child and approves the comment but gives precious time for reflection and elaboration.

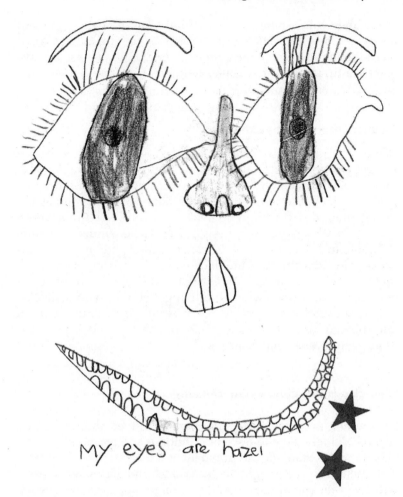

Figure 3.10 Lucy's self-portrait

There are many advantages to this kind of open-minded environment. When children are willing to offer ideas, however
mistaken, there are more ideas available to them or the group.
Children articulating a wide range of ideas are more likely to
hit upon those ideas which explain some or many features of a
phenomenon.

Inviting children to articulate their thinking cannot begin too
early, for even where children lack the ability to express their

ideas they will become familiar with the question, its format and its expectation. In Sasha's case (Cameo 2), inviting her to explain her thinking revealed a misunderstanding of the set task but also gave confirmation of her ability to infer, of her number concepts and of her ability to add.

Encouraging reflective thinking

There is a growing debate on whether young children can be taught to think reflectively. Readers might try encouraging children's reflective thought and come to their own conclusions. First, children can be alerted to the fact that they are skilful thinkers by being praised accordingly: 'Great conclusion – I think you're right!'; 'That's a good hypothesis!'; 'That's a better idea than mine – I thought it was because . . .'. Their critical thinking skills can be developed with the same technique: 'I can see you're thinking . . .'; 'What a clever thought! How did you think of that, I wonder?' and 'I see – when you thought about it you realized it might not work.' We need to volunteer the information that we are thinking, too: 'I've thought of something,' and 'I just can't think why it does that. Can you?'

The classroom context for thinking

Supporting an ethos where 'thinking' is valued throughout the school will take time to develop. Children and teachers will contribute to the changing environment and it is *best* done over time. Children who are taught to be critical and challenge ideas – whether other children's or adults' – might appear to be 'cheeky' or discourteous. Children need opportunities to challenge alongside reminders about the protocol of enquiry. Evaluating and valuing their own and others' ideas is important in creating an atmosphere of enquiry and debate.

Resources

Familiarity with phenomena can sometimes limit imagination and creativity and induce passive responses: 'It always does that!' However, greater familiarity may put severe limitations on a thinker's hypothesizing, knowing that the theory will have to explain all aspects of a complex phenomenon. 'I don't know why. Somebody will know the answer so I'm not going look stupid and say what I think!' The balance is in exploring the familiar and the unfamiliar.

Collections of interesting objects from home or around school are useful stimuli, kept in shoe boxes or other containers, clearly labelled *'For Sorting'* or *'For Classifying'*. This signals to children that collections can be sorted by a variety of criteria, at any time, and that these criteria can change according to circumstances.

Some collections will include objects that may not share immediately identifiable characteristics:

- Pencil, crayon, toy car, cup, chalk, paintbrush, teddy
- Saucepan, mirror, spoon, sock, scissors, apple, wooden brick

Some collections will include objects that demonstrate action and require explanation or suggest investigations:

- Ping-pong ball, airflow ball, tennis ball, football, baby's soft ball, ball of modelling clay
- Bath toy, plastic boat, smooth piece of wood, large pebble, potato, Unifix cube

Some collections may include pictures or card settings to illustrate phenomena or generalized concepts:

- Pictures of bonfire, volcano, iceberg, snowman, cows in a field + real saucepan, tea bag, hot water bottle, ice cube, shell, thermos flask
- Pictures of electric cooker, lawn mower, refrigerator, car, a house + real battery-operated toy, wind-up toy, water pump, scissors, book

A collection of unusual items will surprise children and set off enquiries. It takes time to collect but it encourages wonderful child-parent-teacher collaboration.

At other times, children may need collections with recognizable characteristics and parameters. Comparisons and conclusions can be drawn from two, three or four different objects (big, middle-sized, small; smooth, not-smooth, very rough). There are good reasons why traditional stories adopt this strategy, be it *Goldilocks and the Three Bears* or *The Three Billy-Goats Gruff*. It is easier to draw conclusions from objects with clear demarcations.

Offering extra examples to the children when sorting can:

- confirm conclusions;
- vary the detail slightly;
- contradict the conclusions and challenge the children's thinking.

For example, resources for floating and sinking might include definite floaters (corks, plastic ducks) and sinkers (stones, keys on a key-ring). The introduction of apples, empty yogurt pots and closed plastic bottles half-full of water will draw attention to *where* objects float, *suspension* in water and the *effect of changing conditions*.

Books, both fiction and non-fiction are an excellent way of reinforcing thinking skills. Titles such as *Goldilocks and the Three Bears* (traditional), *The Very Hungry Caterpillar* (Carle 1970) or *The Story of the Little Mole Who Knew it Was None of His Business* (Holzwarth and Erlbruch 1989) can be used to enquire what is happening and why, what will happen next and *how the children know this*. Places also stimulate enquiry, such as museums, farms, working mills, or planetaria, particularly if questions have been planned in advance for children and adults.

The same stimuli for exploration and investigation also encourage interpretations, explanations and critical thinking. Practical resources which encourage children's reasoning must make it possible for them to draw clear conclusions. That means selecting stimuli that have observable reactions or changes: liquid batter turning into solid pancakes, very strong magnets, equipment with transparent sides and slow- as well as fast-moving toys. Living things must include plants that grow very quickly, such as beans or amaryllis flowers, and animals that stay still long enough to be observed, such as woodlice, spiders and snails.

Display

Tabletop displays of objects stimulate classification and enquiry. Children can take turns each day to choose the sorting criteria in containers or hoops. Two folded sentence cards with the name space blank encourages interaction:

.... sorted the objects this way.
Can you guess why .... sorted them like this?

Keep a collection of folded card names to ride the sentence cards like a saddle: Peter, John, Alex, Marcial, Emily, and so on (see Figure 3.11).

Figure 3.11   A folded sentence card with interchangeable name cards encourages interaction

Figure 3.12   'Look! That's what we found out.'

Make displays of recorded results such as graphs and drawings (see Figure 3.12).

Where children have recorded science work in individual books, photocopy some of their work for mounting and general display. Good work is often lost to view in books when it could be the subject of admiration. Always include a question or questions in the display inviting viewers to interpret the findings and make comparisons with their own situation:

The amaryllis grew 2 centimetres (cm) on Wednesday, 1 February.
How many centimetres did it grow on Friday, 10 February?
Which day did it grow 3cm?
How tall was it when it went into flower?
Do you have any bulbs growing at home?

Classroom and other items can stimulate thinking: mechanical toys, pencil sharpeners, egg whisks and musical instruments. Read or tell stories about the great thinkers – scientists and inventors – can serve the same purpose: Nobel, who invented dynamite, Pasteur and vaccination. Make sure that thinkers from different countries and cultures are represented – for example, Ptolemy (astronomy) and Takaki (his dietary changes rid the Japanese navy of beriberi). Encourage the children to describe what life was like before thinkers had invented paper, pencils, water taps, inside flushing toilets, televisions, telephones and computers. Ask the children to evaluate the good and bad effects these inventions and discoveries have had on us and our lives.

Children can draw pictures of themselves as thinkers (Fisher 1990) and explain what might be going on inside their heads. Measuring the children's head circumferences and comparing this with adult measurements impresses children as to brain capacity!

Debate and discussion

Set up classroom and school debates. Children who become confident in class debates can challenge other classes, or the parents. 'Fun' or semi-serious invitation debates could be initiated as follows: 'Class 2 proposes that we should dig up half the playground and plant some trees and bushes. We challenge another class who disagrees with this to debate with us next "Thinking Day"'.

Encouraging thinking at school level can be achieved by giving children a voice on a school council. Each class, from Reception to Year 6 could choose two representatives and attend with their teacher when school-wide issues are addressed, such as, 'How can we reduce the litter in our school?' or 'How can we make dinner play more fun for children and grown-ups?' or 'Can we think of more healthy, tasty food for school dinners?' Meetings once a term could be preceded by classroom surveys of opinions and children will learn that their thoughts and ideas are acceptable and valued and can influence their school environment. Parent representatives and governors could join such meetings or be given the minutes or conclusions of the 'council' in a school newsletter. Children trained this way become informed and responsible citizens.

Finally, speakers can be invited into school assembly, particularly speakers who can inform and respond to arguments about issues. Representatives from Care for the Aged, the Royal Society for the Protection of Birds, the Woodland Trust or a local group trying to reduce traffic/cars/accidents around the school are all available. Preparation would include children thinking of questions in advance.

Assessment

1 Do the children use subjective or objective criteria for sorting?
2 Do the children explain their criteria, and justify items that are excluded?
3 Do the children use observed evidence to describe simple patterns or cause and effect relationships?
4 Do the children use drawings, tables and graphs to present results and use these to draw conclusions?
5 Do the children offer explanations using existing evidence and previous experience?
6 Do the children offer alternative explanations for the same phenomenon?
7 Do the children reflect on their thinking?
8 Do the children know that they think? Do they attempt to explain how?

Summary

Young children's thinking develops from the subjective to the objective; from inductive to deductive thinking. Objective thinking is organizational, rational, creative and critical. Thinking can be actively encouraged. Children need regular practice in classifying and need to be taught how to come to conclusions based on evidence; recording results can help this. Children need opportunities and support to help them hypothesize and begin to think critically. Teachers and classroom stimuli are of crucial importance in developing children's thinking skills.

Questions to ask

1 How can you create more opportunities for children to classify in a variety of ways?
2 Observe or tape record yourself during a science activity or during a school day. How often do you ask the children to interpret or draw conclusions?
3 How often do you ask 'What makes you think that?' or 'I wonder why . . . ?'
4 How could you incorporate a set period each week for 'Thinking Time'? (Different things to think and talk about: topical or seasonal events, issues like traffic on the road or keeping pets, looking after babies or old people.)
5 Can you think of curiosities (objects or toys) to surprise the children into thinking in the home area, on a display table, for measuring or drawing?

4

'I know why bees are furry. Do you?': knowledge and understanding

Cameo 1

After studying bees for two weeks, all the Year 2 children are asked to think of questions and these are typed into a class book. The book is left on display for children to reply to the questions anonymously. Later, the questions are used as starting points for research (see Figure 4.1) (spellings are the children's).

Cameo 2

A Year 5 class is investigating kitchen chemicals, testing lemon and orange juice, baking soda and so on. Colour changes in boiled red cabbage water indicate levels of acidity.

Lisa:	The lemons were the most acid and the vinegar was too.
Tracy:	The sodium bicarbonate was the greenest – less acid.
Lisa:	What colour would it go if we did a mixture of lemon juice and bicarbonate?
Teacher:	What do you think?
Lisa:	Maybe they'll cancel each other out?
Teacher:	You'll have to try it and see. Can you think of anything else that might be acid?
Ben:	Car battery? That's acid.
Teacher:	Good. Anything else?
John:	We could collect the rain.
Teacher:	What makes you think the rain is acid?
John:	It's on the telly. 'Acid rain'.
Ben:	[ignoring the lemons] You can't eat acids anyway.
Teacher:	Why not?

Why are bees furry?   (Kevin)

ro arroct ·
Ladys

becquse it helps
h hem Sting
to keep them warm
to make them look
nice

Why do they fly?   (Phanos)

If they didt the
bag tate carys the
nectar ~~████~~ would
drag onThe ground

Figure 4.1   Children's questions and children's answers

Ben: It's on TV. That man clutching his stomach – 'instant
            pain relief from acid stomach' or something.
Teacher: I think the tablets are really 'anti-acid'.
Lisa: Like anti-clockwise? Does your stomach go all acid
            when you're sick?
Teacher: I'm not sure. How can we find out? From home? The
            library? CD-ROM?

Introduction

What do these children actually *know* about their world? Is there
any evidence of conceptual understanding? How did the children acquire these ideas? Is there any evidence of these children
'wanting' to know? What were the teachers' learning objectives?

How had the teachers stimulated the children to express their ideas? What can teachers do when they do not know the 'right answer'?

This chapter looks at enquiry and the acquisition of knowledge. The nature and sources of knowledge are discussed alongside the desire to know. Children construct their own individual, 'original' concepts which can sometimes create misconceptions. Teachers can encourage the acquisition of knowledge and understanding.

Curiosity or the desire to know

Enquiry-based learning requires a focus. That focus is the desire to know something. 'Wanting to know' has been with us from the dawn of time. We are equipped to explore our environment with delicate sense organs, a complex nervous system and a brain that allows us to interpret and store the collected data: 'It has been estimated that, in a lifetime, a human being can learn up to 15 million items of information' (Asimov 1984: 4).

The desire to know serves many purposes, from positive investigation (to see which wheat grain gives the greatest yield) to the negative activities of the paparazzi invading people's privacy. The desire to know can lead us from knowledge needed for survival to knowledge for its own sake. We want to know 'Is this food fresh?' and 'How did birds evolve?' Wanting to know the answers to big questions has created myths and legends, religions and philosophies. Wanting to know is the hallmark of a learner – curiosity prevents us from stagnation or complacency, but it can be crushed or driven underground all too easily (de Bóo 1987a).

The value of knowing

The acquisition of knowledge has an important influence on our lives. Knowledge can be shared and communicated, by speech and in other ways. Sharing knowledge has been a survival mechanism for our species – perhaps even cave paintings were a teaching aid. Knowledge can also have negative connotations: knowledge of failure or inadequacy, knowledge of lost opportunities. However, most knowledge is a positive thing:

- Knowledge empowers us: we know how to make appropriate responses, control situations and sometimes ourselves.
- Knowledge can make us effective in cooperative problem solving: writing a school policy for equal opportunities; finding solutions to air pollution.
- Knowledge can help us enjoy life: a Bach fugue or a TV quiz game.
- Knowledge raises our self-esteem and gives us self-confidence.
- Knowledge commands respect: we have expertise, gain promotion.
- Most importantly, knowledge, when it is stored in the memory and available for recall, makes us who we are. Knowledge creates our identity (DeLoache and Brown 1987).

Types of knowledge
Knowledge is constantly changing as time and technology modify our experiences and perceptions. There are five different kinds of knowledge: *knowing that* (content), *knowing why* (explanatory), *knowing how to* or working knowledge, *'pure' knowledge* and metacognition or *'knowing that we know'*.

Content knowledge tells us about ourselves and the objects and phenomena of our world. For example, if we drop a wine glass in mid-air, we know that:

- it will fall to the ground;
- it will probably smash;
- it will cut our skin and we might bleed if we handle the glass shards carelessly;
- the wine glass cannot be mended (see Figure 4.2).

Explanatory knowledge tells us the 'why' of things, explaining why objects and living things in our environment behave as they do. For example, we know that:

- there is a gravitational force which pulls objects towards the centre of the Earth;
- glass is a fragile material which will break if dropped on the ground;
- humans have blood vessels under their skin and bleeding is a part of the healing process.

Working knowledge of 'how to' or 'what to' do tells us, for example, how to drive a car or what to do if your fingers are cut and bleeding.

Figure 4.2   The effect of gravity on a wine glass!

'*Pure*' *knowledge* is usually non-functional, such as knowing that the word 'alkali' comes from the words '*Al quali*', used by seventh-century Arabian scientists, or that the wine glass we just broke was an early Victorian champagne flute.

Metacognition is knowing that we know (or don't know). For example, I know that:

- I know how to attend to cuts and bruises;
- I know very little about Victorian wine glasses!

Knowledge as a construct

Knowledge does not exist as a separate entity, awaiting collection like a harvest of hazelnuts. Nor is knowledge a latent entity in the mind waiting, like Sleeping Beauty, to be woken up. Knowledge does not exist until someone has 'thought' it and shared it. Knowledge comes into existence when our minds encounter an object or phenomenon and an idea is born, 'an indissociable subject-object relation' (Furth 1969: 74). Further interactions with the environment continue to modify our ideas.

Knowledge has to be structured into a framework which itself is subject to restructuring. Piaget (1978b) used the term 'assimilation' for taking in new information, and 'accommodation' for the adaptation of previous ideas and restoration of equilibrium. In the absence of any existing structure, children like Lisa in Cameo 2 will construct a new mini-theory to explain the phenomenon (Claxton 1993a).

For example, I may tell you that Chloe has an ulcer. Now you *know* this. You know that Chloe is a female name, 'has' means 'possessing' and you know about ulcers. You still don't *know* who Chloe is or what kind of ulcer she has. If I tell you now that Chloe is a cat, your mental representation will make a big shift from human to family 'pet'; associated emotions and so on. If I go on to say Chloe is a lion in a safari park, your mental concept shifts again. With each new piece of information, the response is to adapt to a new perspective.

Mental constructs
The complexity of the learning process cannot be reduced to a single theory but there is widespread support for the view that children acquire their knowledge through direct exploration of their environment and interaction with people in social and cultural contexts. Mental constructs are the result of purposeful communication and meaningful practical activities. For example, 5-year-old Indira, exploring fruit, points to the apple and says, 'Poisonous.' 'No, it's fresh,' says the teacher. Later Indira says, 'That side,' and five minutes later adds, 'Cinderella,' in a series of thoughts linking reality with a fairy story (Snow White).

If we accept the theory, then *knowing* is a dynamic activity, and 'conceptual development is a continuous, active, creative process [and] nothing remains static or unchanged' (Harlen 1996: 13).

The creation of individual knowledge often results in a variety of constructions or ideas, 'alternative conceptions' or 'frameworks' (Driver *et al.* 1985). Children can hold several conceptions of the same phenomenon at the same time (Driver 1983). Many of these ideas or conceptions will take firm root in individual thinking and be difficult to dislodge or modify. Sometimes fragments of knowledge lie apparently dormant for long periods of time before being brought into use, as in Cameo 2.

Some alternative conceptions are derived from direct experience, some from formal instruction and others from cultural, everyday or social learning (Ross and Sutton 1982; Russell 1993). A child may know from personal experience that the sun moves and the Earth stays still; know from class teaching that the Earth rotates around the sun; and know the sun as anthropomorphic in the song: 'The sun has got his hat on and he's coming out to play'. A child in a different culture may know the sun as a God, subject to appeasement or honour from humans.

The context of knowledge
For young children, knowledge cannot be dissociated from the context in which it has been experienced and this prescribes their knowledge of that concept, as Bansi's experience of eating a lot and getting fat is associated with being pregnant:

Teacher: So what happens when we eat food?
Jenny: It goes down to your feet.
Teacher: It goes down to your feet?
Bansi: If you eat a lot you get fat.
Teacher: You get fat?
Bansi: And then you have a baby.
Teacher: Does everyone have a baby?
Theo: No, only ladies.
Teacher: Why do you think that eating a lot makes you grow a baby?
Bansi: Well, my mummy eats a lot and *she's* growing a baby.

Children require experience of concepts in a variety of contexts before the knowledge can be decontextualized. My young daughter avoided mushrooms for years because she was sick once after eating a mushroom omelette. It took lots of persuasion to convince her to try them again, and again, and accept that mushrooms *per se* were not as bad as she feared!

In science, the context can dictate the theory. Scientists have spent years studying the behaviour of light. In some contexts, light behaves as if it consists of particles; in others, as a wave. For now, we have to accept that light behaves in both ways, and what we choose to observe depends on the context.

Children will also construct their knowledge from informal pieces of information, like the children in Cameo 2. This information is often received in a random or non-directed way from newspapers and books, television, radio and overheard conversations (Black and Lucas 1993). These fragments of knowledge are put together to make sense of unfamiliar situations and reinforce individual constructions and alternative conceptions or misconceptions. Unless challenged these misconceptions may persist. I overheard an older man talking to his wife on the train about 'drinks down the pub'. He told her, 'The alcohol's all to do with sugar – the stronger the alcohol, the sweeter the drink.'

Individual knowledge is often associated with feelings, regardless of the objectivity of the contexts. In education, we often see evidence of this: if children 'know' or believe themselves to be poor in a subject area, they perform less well (Holt 1968), whereas children who are told that they are successful 'know' that they can succeed and usually do. Children who are 'known' as trouble-makers very often live up to the title. It requires considerable experience of success and failure for children to know that their self-worth is more important than any context.

We are usually unaware of how our knowledge has been acquired but it can be seen from the above that knowledge cannot be value-free or culture-free.

It is important to make our children knowledgeable. Our children's intelligence is likely to be measured by how much *knowledge* they can recall in an examination. Traditionally, such tests pay more attention to assessing recalled knowledge than *understanding* of the subject. A vast memory for facts is different from a more limited ability to recall facts but good skills in selecting information and applying it. Understanding is a different kind of knowledge.

Knowledge and understanding

Understanding is knowing how to apply knowledge in different situations, and knowing how to select the appropriate knowledge to use and apply. For example, knowledge of mathematics is needed to respond to either of the following:

(a) $71 -$
     $\underline{26}$
     $=$

(b) What are the factors of:
     $6x^2 - 4x - 10$

You either know or don't know what to do (subtract; factorize).

Similarly, in science, the following question requires knowledge: What change takes place as water approaches and goes below 0°C? You either know or don't know that water expands as it freezes into ice and occupies a greater volume.

Both knowledge and understanding are needed to solve the following problems:

- Jack and Jill's bucket held 31 litres of water at the well. When they fell down the hill 20 litres spilt out. If the children and their parents drink 3 litres each per day, will Jack and Jill have to go back up the hill again today?

• Mary liked cold drinks. She put a bottle of wine and a bottle of milk into the freezer. What did she find the following day?

In these situations, recalling knowledge learnt by rote is not enough. Solving these problems requires language, analytical skills and interpretation. The questions require knowledge of different materials, units of measurement and an ability to predict. Selecting and applying that knowledge is what we term 'understanding'. The following shows how 5-year-old children, discussing a picture of a baby crawling towards an electric cable, knew about but did not understand electricity.

Jon:	No! He might pull the wire out!
Robbie:	The daddy will be cross.
Teacher:	Why's that?
Kari:	'Cos the iron won't work.
Jon:	Baby might get electric shock.
Kari:	You die.
Teacher:	Why? What's in the wires to make you die?
All three:	Electricity.
Teacher:	What's electricity?
Jon:	It's invisible.
Teacher:	How can electricity hurt you?
	[A long pause]
Kari:	You have to switch it off.

Children's development of knowledge

There is some difference of opinion on what triggers development of knowledge and understanding (Mischel 1971; Piaget 1978a). If changes in the child are a natural development from concrete to abstract stages of thought, then learning is an individual process and will occur without adult intervention. However, if learning itself leads to developmental change (Vygotsky 1986), appropriate, timely intervention or 'scaffolding' can facilitate and advance children's learning (Bruner *et al.* 1956). Children do appear to be eager, active thinkers and learners, deliberately trying to make sense of their world, seeking knowledge (Tizard and Hughes 1984) and initiating enquiries which are independent of their ages and stages (Wood 1997).

Children learn in the first instance from practical experience and social interaction. As children mature, practical activities alone are not sufficient to challenge and modify their ideas (Driver *et al.* 1985). If the practical activities are completely unstructured, the children will be expected to find everything out for themselves, including the strategies for finding out. Unstructured enquiry may be appropriate for very young children but primary children might misconstrue some phenomena, develop disconnected ideas and spend time 'going down blind alleys'.

Teachers need to challenge children to research as well as engage in practical enquiries. Not every child has to be stung to know that bees sting (Cameo 1) and it is difficult to give children firsthand experience of animal reproduction in a primary classroom. Children need access to the collective, shared experiences which form the various bodies of knowledge (Cameo 2). Nevertheless, it would be a mistake to preclude children, particularly older children, from having the opportunity to learn by experience: 'Effort, struggle and practice are necessary processes en route to mastery' (Wood 1997: 29).

However knowledge is acquired, it is crucial to recognize that children have developed ideas or concepts about themselves and their world long before they are taught about these ideas in school.

The teacher's role

Attitudes and the desire to know

Wonder
I wonder why, I wonder why,
I wonder why I wonder,
I wonder why I wonder why
I wonder why I wonder.

(Feynman 1986: 48)

Most children enter mainstream school with their desire to know still intact. Children whose appetite to learn is well established are usually a pleasure to teach and easily motivated. Occasionally, children's curiosity will have been suppressed or limited by lack of stimuli and they may be apathetic (Fisher 1990) or uncooperative. Sometimes older children control their curiosity under the impression that showing curiosity is naive, or unacceptable to their peers. In these cases we must try to revive children's interest.

Encouraging children's desire to know is a question of attitude as well as setting tasks in the classroom. Curiosity is contagious and children can catch it! Teachers who peer inside objects, look under leaves and declare, 'I wonder how many seeds this one will have?' are giving strong messages that it is acceptable for children and adults to show curiosity. It is not helpful to *pretend* to be curious – children can sense the difference. However, children value our sharing in *their* curiosity, discoveries and theories.

Children with low interest can be motivated to want to learn (Raper and Stringer 1987). Valuing knowledge for its own sake can be reinforced as a general principle. Fiction and non-fiction books like *The Secret Garden* (Hodgson-Burnett 1911) or *What is a Fish* for the children to read or be read to can inspire curiosity and subsequent enquiry. Project work and questions can set off a search through books, encyclopaedias and CD-ROMs as well as an investigation or survey. It is interesting to think that the better we teach our children to be curious the more questions they will ask and the fewer answers we are likely to have!

Teachers' own knowledge

Teachers need to feel confident in knowing what to teach as well as why and how to teach and how children learn. Currently, primary teachers are expected to be knowledgeable in all or most areas of the curriculum and very knowledgeable in one or two. There can be few professions which demand both breadth and depth of knowledge in so many areas. SCAA (1994) discovered that primary teachers are less confident in some areas of knowledge (science and technology) than others (maths and english). Apart from courses of study, one of the chief methods of gaining knowledge and understanding is by researching and *teaching* the concepts in question.

It is important to remember that teachers have, or are acquiring a wide range of knowledge that transcends subject matter. Teachers know:

- their children;
- their own and the school's educational goals;
- how children learn (younger children need more experiential learning than older children);
- what to teach; in particular, statutory obligations and recommended concepts and skills;

- how to teach (using strategies, models and analogies);
- how to manage the children's learning and use a variety of contexts and resources to encourage this to take place (Harlen 1997).

Teachers need a knowledge base that links concepts and theories to objects and events that are relevant and immediate to primary children and their everyday lives (Bradley 1966). This is usually an area of strength in primary teachers and worthy of self-esteem, as with this student teacher:

> I realise that some of the background knowledge I already have can be a great asset as long as I use it . . . I do not need to know lots and lots about all the different topics we could cover. If I feel weak on a certain subject (which I quite often do) there are plenty of books and other resources which I can use to help me . . . The most important thing I have learned is that if I, as a teacher, am enthusiastic about teaching [science], then the children will see this and some of the enthusiasm will rub off.
>
> (Knowles 1993: 15)

The curriculum can be taught as if it were an unchanging body of knowledge, and this can give a false impression. For example, if science is treated as 'the truth' then children (and adults) will be discouraged from questioning or challenging its ideas (Claxton 1993b). Knowledge without challenge would stagnate.

Knowledge for children

'Knowledge taught in school can be either a tool or a straitjacket . . . either a means by which [a child] actively makes sense of the world or a source of mystification and discouragement' (Barnes 1976: 82). What knowledge is important for children being brought up in a pluralist, Westernized urban environment? In particular, what do we want our children to know and understand about themselves and their world?

Primary teachers in state schools have a specified, obligatory curriculum content, although this is subject to change. Specific learning objectives are given in the National Curriculum (DfE 1995), the Scottish Curriculum (Scottish Office 1993) and international documents (UNESCO 1993). These are broken down into greater detail in long- and mid-term planning documents written by local authorities or school staffs. What to teach is defined, along with when to teach it and, occasionally, how to teach it. Published schemes of work structure the content according to authors' views of which knowledge is appropriate for children at different stages of development. This should make life easier for the teacher, although the enormous quantity of knowledge to be imparted in any one year is rather overwhelming. There is a common perception of curriculum overload (SCAA 1994).

The main reason given for prescribing essential knowledge and skills for primary children is that of entitlement. Theoretically, all children should have access to the chosen areas of learning that society deems as important. The greatest disadvantage of prescribing the curriculum is that of scale and quantity. If we try to include everything, children and teachers are overwhelmed, but if we leave things out children's opportunities are restricted.

In the current global community that relies on fast communication and data-handling, the chief emphases are on language and mathematics. However, sacrificing holistic or other curricular learning to concentrate exclusively on literacy and numeracy is not satisfactory either. Skills in these areas have to be developed but must be applied across the curriculum if understanding is the objective. Neither mathematics nor language can take the place of knowledge of the world nor encourage the wonder of it all.

Most educators from all sectors are united on the need to give children access to the 'big ideas'. For example, we want our children to know:

- what being alive means (see Cameo 1);
- what the world is made of (see Cameo 2);
- what happens when daytime turns into night;
- what makes a light-bulb work;
- what makes a ball bounce, and so on.

We want our children to know how to:

- observe, using their senses;
- measure and check their measurements;
- make plans and decisions;
- conclude and hypothesize;
- record and communicate;
- behave safely;
- cooperate with others;

- behave sensitively towards living things and the environment;
- be self-critical; and
- share their curiosity and enthusiasm with others.

We also want our children to:

- know that they know (Robinson 1983); and to
- know how to learn.

Learning objectives: lesson planning
Perhaps the single most important factor in helping children to acquire knowledge is the teacher's ability to identify the learning purpose. We need to define what we want children to know about, or know how to do. There is no guarantee that children will learn this, but teaching is clearer and more purposeful. Being able to specify the learning purpose requires professional knowledge and skill, acquired from teaching programmes, tutors and class teachers, national documents, schemes, books and from teaching itself. These sources of reference, together with knowledge of how children learn, help us to choose appropriate and relevant learning objectives, such as:

- sorting and classifying mixed materials by their properties;
- observing the effect of heat on ice, candles and chocolate.

These objectives then need further refining and tailoring to the needs of the children. Each of the above objectives contains more than one concept. What does 'mixed' mean? What does 'effect' mean? Selecting the emphasis depends on what we know about our children. 'Knowing how to sort and classify' may be more important than 'knowing the properties of materials'. 'Knowing how to observe' may need more reinforcement than 'knowing that some materials melt easily'. It is as important to focus on 'knowing how to' as it is to focus on 'knowing that'.

Teachers' questions also need to be tailored to the learning purpose (see also Chapter 5). In enquiries, open questions are needed more than closed ones. A focus on 'sorting and classifying' would need 'Which things could go together? Why do you think that?' A focus on melting would require 'What's happening to the wax? What might happen to chocolate if we heat it? Why do you think that?'

Trimming the learning objective like this might appear to be fragmenting the big ideas but this is not so:

The essential interconnectedness of ideas or concepts, skills and attitudes is not denied by focusing on each one at a time [it is simply a way of] looking at different facets of a whole, just as we can look at different faces of a solid without turning it into something two dimensional.

(Harlen 1996: 66)

There are also other factors to be considered. Let us imagine that a lesson is focused on the idea that 'darkness is the absence of light'. Questions influencing the learning purpose will include:

- How old are the children?
- Have the children had experience of light and darkness in a variety of contexts?
- What do individual children know about it?
- Are all the children confident in the language of lesson delivery?
- What resources do we have in school?

After taking these factors into account, we are in a position to narrow the focus still further. Will we concentrate on:

- Darkness?
- Absence?
- Light?

Each word is a concept in its own right. Focusing on one will still refer to the others but the learning objective is clearer, more achievable and assessable (see the discussion on classroom context in the next section).

Because it can be an effective method of reinforcing knowledge and understanding, selecting specific objectives is a good classroom strategy too. Children can be given different aspects of a topic or phenomenon to study and report back or explain their results to the rest of the class. Furthermore, first- and second-hand experience of a concept in several contexts will help children's understanding.

Dealing with questions and misconceptions
In most cases, teachers are teaching children knowledge with which they are familiar. Where children's curiosity or need to know requires an immediate response, teachers have to decide whether to tell children the 'right' answer. For example:

'How long will it take the snowdrop bulbs to grow?'
'About four months.'

Sometimes, a teacher does not know the answer or chooses to withhold some information so that children can construct their own ideas. In these cases, we can stimulate children's explanations, or suggest research (Cameo 2). Sometimes we need to state 'I don't know.' This does not always feel satisfactory but it becomes an important learning opportunity for children. First, they learn that it is acceptable 'not to know'. After that, children:

• initiate the search enquiry;
• become the knowledgeable experts;
• communicate the information;
• learn how to learn, independently.

Following up enquiries takes time but the effort is worthwhile. The classroom is seen as a place of enquiry where questions are valued (Cameo 1) and given resources and support.

Occasionally, children will make statements that teachers know are likely to be untrue or incorrect, as in Cameo 2 when Ben declared that 'you can't eat acids'. Saying 'You're wrong' can destroy confidence. Saying 'Are you sure?' needs to be used with care as children will recognize or assume that you are suggesting that 'they are wrong'. Asking them to explain how they came to that conclusion will help you to check their evidence.

If there is neither the opportunity nor resources available to challenge children's statements or hypotheses at that time, then it is acceptable to say 'It certainly looks like that.' This implies that the evidence supports their theory just like the notion, held for centuries, that the sun revolved around the Earth. What is important is the recognition that the explanation is theoretical and is acceptable 'for now'. Creating opportunities for the child to experience the concept in other contexts can provide challenges to ideas but sometimes this has to be left to other teachers, in other years.

In the enquiring classroom, children and teachers seek knowledge together but there will always be certain differences between the teacher and the learner. The teacher is perceived as the knowledgeable 'expert' and the child is the 'novice'. Generally speaking, teachers move confidently in the areas of their expertise, recognizing and responding to ideas, problems or situations.

They know what the whole picture looks like, or at least more of the picture than the novice. The learner's knowledge is fragmentary, seeing pieces of the jigsaw but not able to perceive the whole (Wood 1988).

Helping children to set up enquiries

The teacher has a role in helping children to 'know how to find out'. This skill equips children for lifelong learning. Knowing how to find out from firsthand experience is fundamental to practical studies (science, technology, music and PE) but can be time-consuming and restrictive. Melting candles, ice and cheese helps children to know about melting; taught information and books can explain the process of melting, change of state and different melting points that can never be tested in the classroom. Knowing how to conduct a search or enquiry and how to access sources of information must occupy an increasing amount of time in a primary child's daily schedule.

Children need challenges, criteria and resources to refine their searches for knowledge. In Cameo 1, the children's questions and answers (hypotheses based on prior experience), prompted by the teacher, formed the basis for research into bees and acquisition of knowledge.

Teachers need to prompt and support the use of secondary sources of information, such as books, although these may not give children precise answers to their questions. Often the questions are too varied or too specific for anything but the largest encyclopaedia, book or CD-ROM to answer. We need to help children to phrase the question and be realistic in obtaining the answer. For example, teachers might ask 'So, what are you going to look up?' and 'If you can't find out exactly, bring back any information you can find.'

In any enquiry, whatever the subject or teaching approach advocated, teaching involves using strategies that help children to structure their own learning. These strategies include the '3 Rs' and 'DIP':

- _Reassuring_ the child: it is OK not to know.
- _Drawing attention_ to significant details: focused questions.
- _Recalling_ the child's previous knowledge or experience: can it be used here?

- *Informing*: giving the child access to knowledge of 'what' or 'how to'.
- *Reminding* the child: of the purpose of the exercise.
- *Praising*: confirmation that the child is successful – knows something new.

Knowing that we know

Children, like the rest of us, are delighted when they know that they know. It excites them into sharing their knowledge in school and at home, from 'Do you know I've got nipples?' (Reception child) to 'There were two magpies, five sparrows, a blackbird and a robin. I could tell by looking' (8-year-old child).

As to knowledge conferring identity, children are unconsciously aware of and enjoy this. At a certain age they will recite or write their name, home number, street, town, region, country and continent, finishing with 'the Earth, the universe'. It is a child's version of Descartes, stating 'I *know* who I am, therefore I *am*!'

Teachers too, should 'know that they know'. Teachers have been trained for their profession. They have subject knowledge, knowledge of how children learn and knowledge of effective strategies to develop that learning; in other words, teachers know how to teach. It is appropriate for teachers to have self-esteem and confidence in their professional standing, and even more, for their expertise to be acknowledged publicly by the community.

The classroom context for knowledge

Attitudes and resources: valuing cultural knowledge

Breaking out of our own cultural perspective is virtually impossible; we are the result of a lifetime of experiences, most of them rooted in one particular culture. An open-minded attitude and awareness of our biases helps us to overcome some of them. We need to establish a classroom atmosphere where multicultural contexts and activities eliminate racism and sexism and value individuals and groups (Bradley 1996).

Science is particularly helpful in generating such an atmosphere. The pursuit of scientific objectivity limits prejudice. Certain scientific concepts, such as 'ourselves' encourage the need for sensitivity to others, value the individual and remind us of our shared characteristics: 'We are all the same' (one species) and 'We are all different' (variation within species).

Children compare their eyes, hair and skin colour – how do they describe themselves? What do they have in common with other children in the class? Comparing arm length and foot sizes will reveal similarities, differences and trends that are culture-free.

Food and diet is an excellent study for acquiring knowledge and awareness. Diverse foods and tools can be explored: okra and mangoes, Irish cheddar and Dutch Edam, pitta bread and bagels, houmous and dhal, a wok, a tava and chopsticks (Peacock 1991). Invite visitors to school to demonstrate and support cooking investigations. One of the most stimulating lessons one Year 3 class had was when a parent came to make Greek pakhlava. We all learned 'about' Greek customs and 'how to' make pakhlava.

Exploring musical instruments gives children opportunities to acquire knowledge about vibration and pitch, materials and their properties, how to play, and ideas about culture and geography. Collect or borrow instruments like a sitar, bamboo pipes, castanets, a sausa (thumb piano) and a tabla.

Stories, poems and illustrated non-fiction provide stimuli for enquiries, for example: stories of life cycles, life in different climates, crystals and gemstones, inventions and discoveries. Children will acquire 'pure' knowledge and knowledge about their world. Books can illustrate knowledge of different cultures and peoples. *Tall Inside* (Richardson 1988) and *Hue Boy* (Mitchell and Binch 1992) are both about children wanting to be taller than they are; one about a White European girl, the other about a Black African boy. The concept is shared by all children and cultures.

It may be necessary to make enquiries of family expectations. Practical class work, particularly in science and technology, treats all children as equal participants but in their home environment there may be cultural differences in the expected behaviour of boys and girls. Teachers must find the balance between creating equal opportunities for all without contradicting family mores and expectations. Often, the children themselves adapt to the different environments – I remember Paulina, an assertive participant by day, a quiet and demure little girl at home time.

Contexts that encourage the acquisition of knowledge and understanding

Children develop understanding when they experience concepts in a range of familiar and unfamiliar situations and activities. For example, the learning purpose may be that 'darkness is the absence of light' and that 'darkness' is the focus. Depending on the age and experience of the children, the kind of activities set up might include:

- setting up a darkened home area with torches or a classroom with blinds;
- discussing fears of the dark and remedies or responses;
- making shadows in the playground or silhouettes in the classroom with an overhead projector;
- counting the number of daylight hours and comparing this with hours of darkness;
- exploring the rotation of the Earth, and time zones around the planet;
- researching and discussing lunar and solar eclipses in the recent past, and in myths and legends.

If the focus is 'light', there is likely to be practical work and discussion about:

- sources of light; candles, torches, room lights, the sun (with safeguards), fireworks, stars;
- colour: painting, contrast, tones, blends, camouflage;
- reflection: of ourselves, objects, light, symmetry;
- refraction and diffraction: in water, lenses and prisms;
- traffic-light signals and semaphore, Morse code, and so on.

The more contexts in which children experience these focuses, the more they move from knowledge to understanding.

Communication

Children need opportunities to share their knowledge with the class, school and local community. Brainstorming approaches can initiate or complete a topic or study in a floor book or display: 'Everything we know about . . .' and 'What we found out about . . .'. Other methods for communicating knowledge and understanding include:

- task discussions;
- end-of-day reporting;
- sharing assemblies;
- written records of discoveries in individual and class books or folders (see Figure 4.3);
- displayed work in the classroom and corridors (see Figure 4.4).

Asking children to prepare a wall or tabletop display can use a variety of skills, and information technology, as well as encourage social skills.

Knowledge and understanding can be communicated in mime or spoken drama. Interpreting a concept in body language can be revelatory to the learner. I have a vivid memory of an experienced advisory teacher, her body working up and down as she tried to convey the behaviour of a water pump. Her face gleamed (with inspiration as well as perspiration!). 'Now I understand water pressure!' she said.

Children need continuous feedback to reinforce their knowledge and self-confidence: 'I can see you really know how to . . .'; 'Your group found out a lot!'; 'You've told me something I never even knew . . . !'

Knowing what children know enables the teacher to:

- give positive feedback to the children themselves;
- inform parents or guardians;
- compare this with school or national expectations;
- evaluate teaching programmes or approaches.

We need to remember that it is not possible to assess *all* the children's ideas and take these into account in our teaching (Harlen 1996).

Assessment strategies

Strategies for assessing children's knowledge and understanding include:

- observation of behaviour/actions;
- verbal responses to questions or volunteered information;
- drawings;
- written work (by hand and word-processed);
- individual and group discussion;

Juliet Roberts
I found out today that wood floats. We found out that cotton wool can float and sink to make it float you can just put it in to make it sink you try to put water in it. We found out that when the wood was in the water it was 340g. plasticene can float What you do is you holow ~~it~~ it out and make the was high
(walls)

and then put it on the water. metal can sink and float too.

Figure 4.3 Juliet's investigation into floating

Figure 4.4 A toothy display: modelling clay and plaster of Paris

- models;
- dramatized accounts (mimed or spoken);
- maths records, including graphs (by hand or computer generated);
- presentations;
- concept mapping (before and after teaching);
- concept cartoons (Keogh and Naylor 1997);
- activities in which children demonstrate their understanding.

It is difficult to assess children's comprehensive knowledge of themselves and their world on a strict scale of 1–10 in paper and pencil tests which often require high levels of skill in English and mathematics. All such tests need to be viewed within a larger framework: children have knowledge which is not revealed in a test and other background factors affect performance: first language, opportunities and experiences, health, attendance and so on. It is important to assess children's skills in practical tasks – regular moderating sessions with colleagues will ensure greater objectivity and reliability of judgements.

It is very difficult to *measure* children's 'desire to know' in any other way than a subjective way, although teachers value this attitude. Indeed, it is an educational goal, whether stated or unstated, that *we want our children to want to know*.

Resources

Children's acquisition of knowledge is very dependent on resources, particularly books, videos, CD-ROMs and other software. The library needs to have high quality materials arranged in an accessible and stimulating way (some practical resources are outlined in other chapters and a basic list is given in the Appendix). This can have implications for budget expenditure. Good information books, software and encyclopaedias cost money.

When a substantial amount of money has been spent on secondary sources of information it is important to invite parents and governors in to see the latest acquisitions. Surround the books or software with questions to which visitors can find answers: 'Can you find out what the larva of a ladybird looks like? How does a mechanical donkey work? What would you find at Giza?'

Better still, combine the book and software exhibitions with:

- a publishers' book sale including information and inspirational books;
- a quiz/'Trivial Pursuit' evening for parents, friends and governors, perhaps with questions prepared by children based on topics recently studied in school;
- a visiting speaker: a scientist, a baker, a photographer, a gardener etc.

Use parents and others as sources of information for topics and project work. Let the children's surveys include families and friends. Invite in people from the community with knowledge and expertise, such as:

- a parent with a baby to show how the baby looks, behaves, what the baby can do and how the family cares for it;
- parents from Cyprus or West Africa to describe their birthplace and what school life is like there;
- parents or others who are bus drivers, switchboard operators, farmers, nurses, police constables etc.

It is particularly important in environments where children have limited experience of a variety of backgrounds to invite people from different cultures who will extend children's knowledge of the world community.

Assessment

1 Do the children show a desire to know or curiosity in objects and phenomena?
2 Do the children persevere with enquiries in the classroom? In school? At home?
3 Do the children volunteer ideas in one-to-one, small group or class discussions?
4 How does the children's knowledge compare with what they knew six months ago?
5 Do the children know they know more?
6 Do the children know that they have improved their skills?

Summary

This chapter has discussed the desire to know and different types of knowledge; knowing that, knowing why, knowing how to, and knowledge of knowing. Knowledge is not value-free.

Understanding is an ability to apply knowledge. Children acquire knowledge from firsthand experiences, social interactions and secondary sources of information. Teachers can provide practical experiences, resources and guidance to aid children's acquisition of knowledge. They can simplify learning objectives to make them accessible without making them simplistic or misleading. Teachers' own attitudes can reassure children that it is acceptable not to know, that no one can know everything. Teachers help children to learn that they can initiate their own enquiries or searches for knowledge and find things out for themselves.

Questions to ask

1 How can you create more opportunities for children to suggest their own searches for knowledge?
2 How can you improve the environment so as to stimulate enquiries?

3 How can you improve the variety, quality and quantity of sources of information?

4 How often do you seek information yourself about subjects? Children? Other?

5 How could you incorporate a set period per week for general feedback: 'Things we found out this week'?

5

'Do you mean what I think you mean?': communication skills

Cameo 1

Year 1 children are exploring an unknown object – an ocarina, a small round clay wind instrument. The teacher asks, 'Can you guess what this is?'

Charlie: I think the holes are for little animals to live in.
Teacher: What a good idea. What made you think of that?
Charlie: I don't know. I never thunk it before!

Cameo 2

Year 4 children watch while an apple floats and a look-alike apple (a Nashi pear) sinks. The teacher asks, 'I wonder why that one sank?'

Jim: It's heavier.
Teacher: Or?
Rick: Maybe the apple's got holes inside it . . .
Sara: You've put a marble inside it!
Teacher: Could be. Anything else?
Toni: It's going rotten?
Alistair: It's the stuff inside. The pear's all squashed up inside [clasping his hands to demonstrate] and the apple stuff is further apart [Pulls his hands apart].
Teacher: You're right – the pear *is* more dense than the apple. Some of the other fruit is dense too [clasps her hands together].

Cameo 3

The arrival of new musical instruments initiates Year 5 children's interest, exploration and enquiries. The teacher's questions 'What can you tell me about this drum?' and 'Anything else?' generate a range of descriptions. The children are then asked to write down their answers to 'How do you think the drum makes a sound?' Answers vary (children's spellings):

> You listen to it and you hear it (Meg).
> Only when you hit it (Justin).
> The air inside the drum makes a big eco and it reches your ears (Pam).
> The vibrashuns from the skin of the drum and you can see it if you look close (Siva).
> When you hit it it makes a big BANG but its only a little bang in yore ears unles yore right up agenst it you shud NOt do it cos you can hurt yore ears (Jack).

Introduction

How did Charlie derive the word 'thunk'? Why did the teacher introduce the word 'dense' when she did? What kind of questions do the teachers use to obtain varied answers? What other strategies could the teacher have used to find out what the children knew about sound?

Enquiring children and challenging teachers will ask questions and negotiate meaning. Language in the context of an enquiry plays a central role in children's understanding of themselves and their world and encourages the child's ability to think. It is important to introduce new vocabulary at the right time and in the right way. Teachers' open-ended questions have an important role in stimulating children's intellectual and practical enquiries.

Communication: negotiated meanings and terminology

Meaningful communication depends on language and mutual understanding. Acquiring language is not simply the acquisition of words with a universally accepted context; words have a unique meaning to each of us arising from our experience, culture and the social conditions in which the words were acquired. We construct our own meanings (Piaget 1929; Driver *et al.* 1985) and then use language to modify our words and expressions to consider or accommodate other meanings.

Try it for yourself. Say the word 'kee' phonetically. What does this word evoke? Does it evoke an identical image for your colleague? Partner? The generally agreed definitions of keys or quays, both real and abstract, were negotiated long ago but individual images of 'keys' will vary.

Communication is possible without speech – for example, using body language, facial expressions and gestures. Enquiries can also take place without speech, particularly at two extremes of learning: infants' experience of their immediate environment and students undertaking literature research. However, for communication with others we need language to discuss observations and questions and this encourages cognitive development (Bernstein 1971; Bruner 1971).

Language not only allows the learner to articulate and consolidate concepts but allows the learner to 'learn'. Children who have acquired language skills can be challenged further to explain and reflect on their explanations (Tough 1973, 1977; Vygotsky 1986). Intuitive ideas left unchallenged can lead to misconceptions (Harlen 1996).

Apart from the difficulties inherent in the acquisition of language and construction of meaning, sometimes the same word or expression can have different meanings – for example, 'Mrs Jones' pet' and 'the vicious dog that bit me' refer to the same animal. This can make teaching and learning both rich and confusing:

In the dialogue between child and adult, both of them may refer to the same object, but each of them will think of it in a different framework. The child's framework is purely situational, with the word tied to something concrete, whereas the adult's framework is conceptual.

(Vygotsky 1986: 133)

Communication can be most confusing in areas such as science and maths where precise language is required and words are used that have other, everyday meanings, such as the word 'force'. As Francis Bacon wrote, 'The ill and unfit choice of words wonderfully obstructs the understanding' (1620, Aphorism 43). Scientific terminology presents difficulties because the words are detached from reality, context or culture. Communication in science requires universally accepted definitions for effective discussion within and across language boundaries. However, this demand for precise terminology can create difficulties for primary children. It can reduce their self-confidence and even alienate older children from science altogether. Finding the balance between precision and fudging the meaning by oversimplification is a delicate skill that teachers practise daily.

Body language and contextual clues

Classroom enquiries and scientific thinking are not totally dependent on the child's *speech*, but are dependent on their understanding of language. Sometimes, children do not speak, perhaps lacking confidence, appropriate vocabulary or familiarity with English as their second language. Children sometimes reinforce their speech or replace it with gestures which are interpretable, and can be checked by the teacher's clarifying questions. For example, Alistair in Cameo 2 used his hands to reinforce his spoken definition. Interpretation depends on positive attention and an awareness of the context of the communication. For primary children, the more language is set in a concrete, practical situation with visible phenomena, the easier it is to interpret the body language offered by teachers or learners.

Acquisition of speech: social and cognitive development

It used to be thought that the acquisition of speech was an outcome of the need to communicate (Searle 1969), something that could be learnt by copying adults. While the need to communicate does constitute a powerful stimulus, it is now thought by many that we are born with an inherent predisposition to learn language. Chomsky (1976) compared mental evolution to physical evolution of the body, that is, that the cognitive structures of the mind are as ready for development as the infant's hands are for motor development and coordination. We are biologically programmed to learn language, whatever the prevailing culture or indigenous language. The theory suggests that the rules and structures of a language are too many and too complex to be learnt simply from instruction or copying:

> Ordinary linguistic behaviour characteristically involves innovation, formation of new sentences and new patterns in accordance with rules of great abstractness and intricacy. This is true both of the speaker, who constructs new utterances

appropriate to the occasion, and of the hearer who must analyse and interpret these novel structures.

(Chomsky 1971: 153)

In Cameo 1, Charlie's creative use of the past tense of 'think' is an illustration of this. Children listen, absorb words and rules and apply them in new, creative ways.

Piaget (1959) theorized that early egocentric speech (talking to oneself out loud) is neither an attempt at communication nor of use in the cognitive process. However, Vygotsky (1986) argued that young children's speech appears to show awareness of people, a problem or actions to be taken and that 'speaking out loud' is the precursor to internalized thought. As such, speech is part of the process of children's cognitive development, a learning tool in itself: 'Talking clearly aids the expression of thinking, and perhaps frequently the very use of talk initiates and refines the child's thinking'. (Tough 1973: 88).

The young child's acquisition of words can be thought of as the acquisition of concepts (Ausubel 1968; Chomsky 1976; Vygotsky 1986). Early words are not clearly defined concepts, they are mental pictures of the concept or 'potential concepts'. Giving something a 'name' is an act of thinking and learning which goes alongside practical exploration and investigation (Sutton 1992) (see Figure 5.1). The acquisition of speech is the start of that long process of reducing the complexity of the world to words and symbols.

Linguistic development

Even where children are confident in the language of the classroom, there are some aspects of an enquiry which cannot be communicated clearly until the child has the necessary vocabulary and syntax. Formulating questions, or offering explanations or hypotheses is impossible without speech. Children cannot define cause and effect relations without prepositional language (Isaacs 1936; Vygotsky 1986). Hypothesizing requires an ability to use three clauses appropriately, linked by the correct use of the word 'because'. For example:

Teacher: What will happen if I light the candle?
Alice: [She droops, demonstrating 'melting'] [cause and effect]
Bronwyn and Colin: Melt. [cause and effect]

Figure 5.1 Articulating ideas clarifies thinking

Teacher:	What makes you think it will melt?
Alice:	[Silence]
Bronwyn:	'Cos it's a birthday one. ['because' not yet fully understood]
Colin:	'Cos the hot of the candle makes it melt. ['because' used correctly + generalization]

Theories of learning have a bearing on children's developing enquiries. Children use their cognitive ability to change sentences into questions without making major errors of language (Chomsky 1976).

Language development requires a wide range of experiences and a linguistic environment where children are exposed consistently to a variety of forms of language on a daily basis (Paul Hamlyn Foundation 1993). These forms are speaking, listening, reading and writing (Moffat 1968) but might include inner speech (Fisher 1990). Furthermore, the 'right question at the right time' (Elstgeest 1985), an appropriate challenge, or 'the first step towards a solution' can support children's development and enquiries (Fisher 1990: 190). Such 'scaffolding' encourages children's thinking and language development. Bruner and Haste (1987: 22) include:

- correcting the child's early utterances
- responding to the child's ongoing commentary
- aiding the presentation of appropriate, comprehensible and increasingly sophisticated accounts of behaviour, which involves concepts, language content and appropriate styles of language use.

Children also need regular, positive verbal approval (Tough 1977).

For children to feel confident, language requires a context in which it is used, and a positive atmosphere. Practical enquiries with interactive and challenging discussions will extend thinking, speech and writing. The role of the teacher is important in creating these conditions for the child (Barnes 1976; Tough 1977; Bruner and Haste 1987).

The teacher's role

Teachers' attitudes have an important influence on the language of enquiry in the classroom. Children will offer more questions, ideas and responses if given opportunity, time and approval (Cortazzi, in press).

Initiating enquiries: the importance of questioning

The first key to wisdom is constant questioning . . . By doubting we are led to enquiry, and by enquiry we discern the truth.

(Peter Abelard 1079–1142)

Finding out what is in the children's heads (Bruner 1971) is one of the reasons why teachers ask questions. Awareness of children's existing skills, knowledge and understanding can assist the teacher in extending their thinking (Ausubel 1968; Harlen 1996). Finding out what the child knows or can do enables the teacher to plan an effective 'next step' in the learning programme for that child or a group of children, as in Cameos 2 and 3.

This assessment is traditionally done by asking questions. Teachers ask a lot of questions: nearly 20 per cent of all teachers' utterances are questions (Galton et al. 1980). Nearly half of these are aimed at class control, getting information, checking that instructions have been understood, or showing interest.

At their best and most productive, teachers' questions can guide and stimulate thinking. Questioning can be called 'good' when it makes cognitive demands on children (Tizard and Hughes 1984). Unproductive questioning is a result of that 'testing reflex' where a teacher feels impelled to ask questions without having thought about the purpose in advance (Jelly 1985). The questions in Figure 5.2 will promote intellectual and practical enquiries, and encourage active exploration, investigation or research. They include and expand the criteria and questions defined originally by Elstgeest (1985: 110).

Most of the questions have other dimensions as well as encouraging and developing language skills. For example, questions that ask children to notice and describe details provide teachers with information about gaps in the children's vocabulary and terminology; problem-posing questions encourage designing and making, motor and social skills.

Neutral questions such as 'Or?' and 'Anything else?' invite alternative responses which suggest to the children that there is more than one reason why things might happen. Children perceive neutral questions as affirming but seeking elaboration or more ideas. Answers are offered by the original child or volunteered by other children, as in Cameo 2. When Reception children were exposed to neutral questions over a few months, the number of alternative responses, both descriptive and explanatory, increased substantially compared with the control group (see Figure 5.3).

Good questioning needs skill and sensitivity (Elstgeest 1985). Questions that respect each child's current abilities and potential need to be pitched at an appropriate level (Tizard and Hughes 1984). A lack of response may not be evidence of a lower level of understanding but may indicate a limited knowledge or a limited understanding of the question (Tough 1973). Questions can highlight the gaps between teacher/pupil understanding, not only resulting from their differing social backgrounds and speech patterns (Bernstein 1971) but from the use of scientific terminology, like 8-year-old David who wrote 'snails got and ten eyes' (antennae).

Open-ended or closed questions?

Classroom discourse is typically controlled by teacher questions that often demand quick, terse, factual answers and

Question type	Examples	Result
Attention-focusing	Have you seen . . . ? Do you notice . . . ? What is it doing? What is inside? What can you tell me about . . . ?	Observation: using the senses
Measuring and counting	How many . . . ? How big is . . . ? What shape is . . . ? Is it longer than . . . ? Are there more . . . ?	Observation: using mathematics (length, area, numbers)
Comparing	Are they alike? How? How many differences? Do any of these belong together? Can you guess why I have put these together? Did it go further than . . . ?	Observation: classification, properties
Eliciting children's questions	How many questions can you think about . . . ? Can you think of 20 questions about . . . ? Which questions can we ask to find out about . . . ?	Raising questions
Planning	Which questions can we try out or investigate? What will you need? How long will it take? What shall we compare? Or measure? How will we know if it's fair?	Planning the investigation
Problem-posing	Can you find a way to . . . ? Can you make it go . . . ? Can you make a . . . ?	Investigation: design and technology, action, problem solving
Thinking and action	What do you think will happen . . . ? What happens if . . . ? Why do you think that will happen?	Predicting: action and investigation leading to hypotheses and problem solving
Recording and communicating	How will we remember what happens? Shall we write it or draw? Shall	Planning and recording; communicating

	we keep a score? How shall we let the others know what happened?	
Interpreting	What happened? Did it do what you expected? What did that tell you? What does the graph tell us? What else could it mean?	Observation; drawing conclusions; interpreting
Hypothesizing	Why do you think it did that? Could there be another reason? Can you explain it to the others?	Hypotheses; communication
Evaluating	Do you need to check or change anything? Is there anything we need to repeat? Would you do it any differently next time? What was the best part of your investigation?	Evaluation; critical reflection
Thinking	What do you mean by . . . ? What do you think . . . ? I wonder whether . . . ? What made you think of . . . ?	Reflection; metacognition
Neutral	Or? Anything else? Anyone else? ('Red?': child's statement turned into a question)	Reflection leading to more observations and explanations
How and why	Why does it . . . ? How does the . . . ?	Difficult and not helpful to ask or answer. Imply that there is a *right* or only answer or a 'correct' scientific *fact*. Ask the questioner for their opinion (i.e. Why do *you* think?)

Figure 5.2 Questions to promote enquiry, investigation and exploration

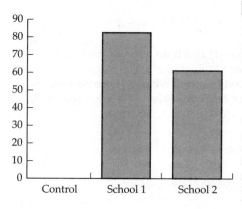

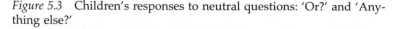

Figure 5.3   Children's responses to neutral questions: 'Or?' and 'Anything else?'

leave little time for children to respond, elaborate or reason out loud. Perhaps this explains, in part at least, why some children do not learn how to express their ideas, formulate their thoughts or say what they know. Furthermore, if the teacher asks all the questions, then he or she dictates the course of events; what will be thought about and when. We have to ask ourselves whether this provides the pupils with opportunities to plan, regulate, reason and explain themselves.

(Wood 1988: 144)

The enormous potential of open-ended questions for encouraging thinking and enquiries make it surprising that this kind of questioning does not dominate classroom discussions. Barnes' studies (in Barnes *et al.* 1986) revealed that questions designed to encourage children to 'think aloud' were very infrequent, and most of the questions led to teachers' preconceived ends. Questions requiring one-word, factual answers or recall of the teacher's earlier statements are defined as 'closed'. In studies by Galton *et al.* (1980), these accounted for 50 per cent of all the questions: 30 per cent requiring factual answers, 20 per cent recalled explanations. Their studies found that only 5 per cent of all questions asked were open-ended.

The differences between the two question types can be exemplified as follows:

The teacher holds up a red box.

Q1: Is this red?	A: Yes.	(Closed questions
Q2: What colour is this?	A: Red.	eliciting one reply)
Q3: What colour does this remind you of?	A1: A pillar box. A2: Blood! A3: My red skirt.	(Open question: many acceptable responses)
Q4: Can you find anything in the room to match this colour?		(Open question: many acceptable responses)

The first two questions require one-word answers, the third seeks recall and mental comparison, the fourth invites action, comparison and classification. The open questions can be answered satisfactorily in a variety of ways and different individual responses can be valued and justified. The open questions in Cameos 2 and 3 produced several responses which led to cutting open the Nashi pear and investigations into sound reflections and echoes, sound vibrations and the ear.

The most common *everyday* reason for asking a closed question is that the questioner does not know the answer. It is an atypical situation when we are asked questions by someone who already knows the answer or at least the answer they want to hear (Wood 1988). Traditional classroom situations can compare with television quiz shows. Teachers ask questions to which they know the answer and generally children try to guess what answer the teachers wish to hear. In some classrooms, teachers choose one child after another until someone gives the 'right' or predetermined answer, with a typical waiting time of one second, before answering the question themselves (Swift and Gooding 1983).

Closed questions with preconceived answers can generate anxiety and loss of self-confidence (Tizard and Hughes 1984), and stifle enquiries. On the other hand, closed questioning can be effective, for example, where retention of facts is important in the short term (Nuthall and Church 1973). Children's questions tend to be closed or prescriptive, although still valuable starting points for discussion or enquiry (see Stephen's questions in Chapter 1, page 14, and Chapter 4, Cameo 1). However, the longer-term effects of open compared with closed questions suggest that pupil achievement is higher when they encounter open-ended questions with a greater cognitive demand (Redfield and Rousseau 1981).

Open-ended questions are more likely to initiate thoughtful enquiries and practical exploration. The use of open questioning in discussion, with its implications for more than one acceptable reply, gives children thinking time even while another child is replying, allowing them to reflect, modify or reword their own responses. Such thinking takes time and effort (Fisher 1990). Sensitive timing and sensitive listening are therefore essential in developing children's thinking.

Listening

Listening is a necessary, positive, active behaviour. Teachers discover what children are thinking and see the world from their perspective (Fisher 1990). Sometimes silent listening is more valuable than talk if teachers 'resist the urge to answer' (Harlen 1996: 112). If children are the only listeners then learning is a unidirectional process (Barnes 1976). Holt (1968) estimated that two-thirds of education is talk, and two-thirds of that is teacher-talk. If children are denied opportunities for interaction in the linguistic and cognitive sense, then, lacking control of the content and strategies, their enquiries close down.

The quality of our listening to children may vary according to circumstances, such as the background noise level, monitoring child X, children's inattention or our need to move the discussion on. Nevertheless, listening is an essential, interactive two-way discussion that values the children's questions and comments. It is truly exploratory in a way that teacher directed discourse is not.

Listening *is* difficult and time consuming, if we are giving concentrated selective attention to one child's speech. It requires a setting which has been organized for safe independent learning. Enquiry-based learning generates discussion or classroom 'noise' and pupil talk is often perceived as synonymous with lack of class control. However, genuine enquiries will usually produce a positive 'sound' where the talk is purposeful and productive, on-task and supportive (Peacock 1991).

Listening teachers and an atmosphere of enquiry tend to make children into good listeners also. They become interested and involved in the enquiries and results and there is an acceptable sound-level of discussion. Such talk is not solely enquiry-focused and I would not wish it to be. It is perfectly possible to be working hard with colleagues or family and at the same time comment on the weather, remind someone of a time constraint or make a joke about the difficulty of the work. Children who are well motivated and intent upon their search for learning operate in the same way.

Interactive discussions are also influenced by the children's homes or cultures. Bilingual children and non-standard English speakers are advantaged by working in an enquiry-based environment. Although the diversity of language and terminology may sometimes confuse, the atmosphere and opportunity to access and use new vocabulary simultaneously with monolingual children has a positive effect (Peacock 1991). Staff who would normally support children's learning are an asset in these practical situations, repeating or translating some of the faster-moving dialogue.

Using new vocabulary

Practical activities involving exploration and investigation are highly effective in encouraging language (Light and Gilmour 1983). Children have opportunities for descriptions and explanations and teachers have opportunities to provide appropriate terminology (Harlen 1996) (see Figure 5.4). Rephrasing the children's words can give them access to the correct terms as with Alistair in Cameo 2. The message is implicit without being overstated.

Children's attention can be focused on the differences in meaning by providing them with a challenge to define as many different sentences or contexts for a particular word or phrase as they can. This makes the children really think about the meaning of the word and its referent. For example:

'May the Force be with you!' (*Star Wars* film)
'He forced me to give him my sweets.'
'I had to force the door open when it was jammed.'
'The force of gravity makes things accelerate towards the Earth.'

The word 'force' can be defined more precisely – for example, an action or reaction which has strength and direction. However, we all use words loosely on some occasions, often qualified with 'You know what I mean'. It is very important to let children have

cold	hot
the batter was liquid first and the colour was creamy.	the pancake was solid and on the pancake there was a spiral
the candle was solid and it was hard and it was made of three colours.	when the candle was hot the wax was liquid.

Figure 5.4 Children's exploration of pancakes cooking and candles melting helped them to understand the terms 'liquid' and 'solid'

this freedom to begin with (Harlen 1996), exploring language before leading them to more precise terms. Teachers can decide when it is appropriate to supply children with the correct term (as in Cameo 2 where the teacher introduced the word 'dense'), and this decision will depend on whether:

- the child has the relevant knowledge and understanding in place;
- the word will clarify or add to the child's understanding at that time (Harlen 1996: 94).

Children (and adults) can find it hard to admit ignorance and may avoid using a word if unsure of its pronunciation. Establishing an atmosphere where new words can be used safely is important. For example, how do *you* pronounce the word 'lichen', that living growth covering damp rocks? Liken or litchen? (Either pronunciation is correct.)

Primary teachers need to understand abstract concepts, such as 'accelerate' or 'dense' and be able to put them into real contexts to give them meaning. This helps children to see how the word refers to significant events or situations in their own experience. A word or expression needs to be experienced in *several* contexts, for only then can a word acquire an abstract meaning for which there is a universal consensus.

Words help us get to grips with invisible or inaccessible abstract ideas, such as 'gravity' or 'digestion'. We model ideas by using descriptive words, analogies and metaphors. There are limitations to such analogies; the analogies may be taken too literally and confuse children and the analogies cannot account for all the characteristics (e.g. electrical flow compared to water flow). Nevertheless it is important for teachers to use these and other models as, even if the analogy is not helpful, the action of teachers trying to make links with children's existing experience has a positive effect on their understanding (Jabin and Smith 1994).

We must encourage children to offer their own models by saying 'What does it remind *you* of?' Their models, if they explain the phenomenon with reasonable accuracy at that time, will have more meaning for them and will be retained better in the memory.

Further strategies to consolidate conceptual understanding include selecting words and asking the children, preferably in small groups, to illustrate their idea in mime or make three-dimensional models or collages. Children negotiate meaning and understanding, and ideas that are communicated in this way are clarified for both actors/artists and audience.

Reading and recording

Reading for information involves critical and creative thinking (Fisher 1990) as children try to make sense of the text and illustrations and reflect on the ideas. Reading for information requires the same skills as reading fiction, although it can be less easy to see the 'storyline' in an information book. For example, 'In spring the plants have flowers. The flowers attract insects. The insects pollinate the flowers. The plant grows seeds. The seeds need somewhere to grow. Some fall onto the ground. Some seeds fly in the air . . .' and so on.

Reading can also make the referent clearer, as when seeing the word written down, like 'key' or 'quay' (see page 107).

Written work
In the present climate, many teachers are reluctant to initiate what appear to be 'time-consuming' enquiries although this

approach leads to better understanding. Teachers are often tempted to feel even more guilty if there is no written record of the task but we need to resist this. Written work is valuable but should be planned and purposeful, not an automatic continuation of every practical activity (see Chapter 2).

All too often, the results of the children's explorations and investigations are written up in one format only, that is, descriptive prose. Sometimes this is appropriate, however, there needs to be a range of options used in recording practical work to avoid the plea, 'Do we *have* to write about it?' Loose requests can have unproductive results, with children writing without a purpose or motivation, as I know from experience!

Writing up an enquiry offers rich opportunities for communication: diaries, descriptions, questions, planning or results of an investigation, using phenomena for stories and poems, notes, drafts, arguments, concept maps, labelled drawings and jokes (see Figures 5.5 and 5.6). Writing can be individual or shared. Other options for recording include: drawings, paintings, diagrams and models; photographs, tape recordings and CD/Internet pictures; mathematical sets and graphs; databases, digitizing and word processing.

All formal work should be part of an ongoing dialogue, principally with the teacher. Teachers can write back on post-it notes or books, affirming, elaborating, informing or challenging the children – for example, 'Good explanation', 'You found out a lot!'. Children learn that the clearer their recordings and explanations, the easier it is for the listener or audience to grasp their meaning and discoveries. Pupils require opportunities to create new meanings by talking, drawing and writing, building new understandings on the foundations of the old (Barnes 1969).

The classroom context for communication

Setting the scene

Children's enquiries need an atmosphere which is non-threatening but *not* non-critical (Raper and Stringer 1987). When children are challenged to reflect and evaluate they modify their ideas. Interactive classroom discussions need settings where all children can have eye contact with the teacher. This occurs when

Insects.........Alexandra

Butterfly,butterfly
Caterpillar,caterpillar
Munching,crunching,
Creeping ,crawling
Sleeping,gnawing
Eating,eating
Meeting,meeting
Sleeping ,sleeping

Bees,bees
Funny little things,
Got nice wings.
Little ladybird,
Little ladybird,
Little spotted dot,

That snail
Went in a pail
Of water.
I saw a lacewing
Pretty thing.
It's green all over
Like a leaf.

Figure 5.5 Poems about animals observed in the playground

teachers stand facing the class (seated at their tables/desks) or sit facing the children sitting on the mat. Debates require children to have eye contact with each other and this means sitting in some form of round, where every child is given equal status.

Creating opportunities for all children to respond will include brainstorming ideas and more open-ended questions. An occasional change of approach, selecting named children to respond to questions, rather than asking for 'hands up' can ensure that all children are involved.

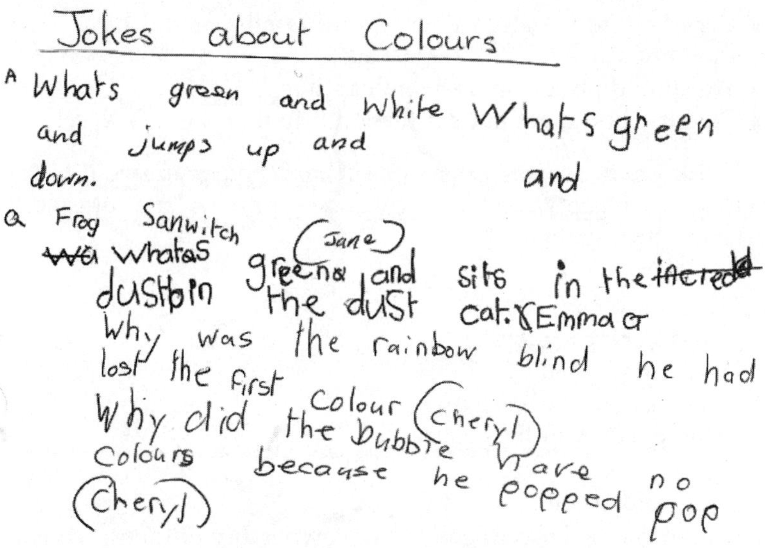

Jokes about Colours

A Whats green and white and jumps up and down.

Whats green and

Q Frog Sanwitch (Jane)

Whatas green and sits in the incread
dustbin the dust cat. (Emma)

Why was the rainbow blind he had
lost the first colour (Cheryl)

Why did the bubble colour (Cheryl)
colours because he have no pop
(Cheryl) popped pop

Figure 5.6 Jokes inspired by an enquiry into colours

Discussion and debate

The classroom can become a genuine 'community of enquiry' (Lipman 1974) if children are encouraged to talk, challenge and debate on a regular basis. This can be a regular part of school life from Year R onwards, in the classroom and at school level. Although this approach to speaking and listening enhances enquiry and critical thinking, it is not used as often as it could be (de Bóo 1988a). Quite young children are capable of arguing a case if the subject matter is chosen with relevance to their experience and interests. Older children become adept and convincing, when given preparation time to research their case and obtain information. Working cooperatively gives children the opportunity to use a range of language formats.

The topics for debate must be appropriate and relevant for the children but not underestimate their capacity to focus their attention on big issues. Classroom debates could include arguments for and against the following:

- We should have chips for dinner every day.
- We should cut down the trees in the wood so we can play ball games there.

- Cars pollute the atmosphere so no family should have more than one car.
- We shouldn't keep animals in captivity.
- Parents should get fined if their children misbehave in school.

While such debates often reveal hardened attitudes ('You're wrong, anyway!') they can generate opinions and questions (Fisher 1990) such as:

'That's not fair.'
'It's different for us . . .'
'What if you can't . . . ?'
'Why should we?'
'Who decided in the first place?'

'Playing with words'

Children can be encouraged to take ownership of their own language and understand its construction by creating vocabulary. Exploring unfamiliar or familiar objects provides children with opportunities to invent names, such as for plants found in the playground: 'prickle-leaf', 'golden star' or 'wobblestalk'. This enquiry can result in voyages of discovery and delight, researching the real names in information books. The enquiry can work in reverse – what is the origin or reason for names such as 'coltsfoot', 'horse tail fern' and 'dandelion'? What are the plants called in Welsh? Bengali? Farsee?

Try asking the children to imagine meanings for real but unfamiliar words like chigger, coprolite, fumarole, and words that are pretend or unreal (as far as we know), such as hengil, diblish, jangleberry. Play the game in reverse and ask older children to think of sentences using words (with or without prefixes and suffixes) with more than one meaning: duck, boot, log, foot, head, scratch. Children can search dictionaries for a range of meanings or work in groups to find a word to challenge the rest of the class.

Children should be encouraged to record their 'playing with words' and ideas on an informal, non-corrected basis in exercise books or a computer folder. 'My Questions', 'Science Notebook' or 'My Thinking Page' can be set up to experiment with ideas, make jottings or write down their results. Some of these might be used as a basis for neat work or word processing or information technology graphing programmes (Barnes 1976).

Encourage the children to invent symbols in the same way as inventing vocabulary and they will begin to understand the reasons behind a unified, agreed approach to symbolic representation. Make sure the children have enough time to draw from reality, recall or imagination – trees, the sea, people, batteries, bulbs, cooking – then develop this by asking them to invent their own 'shorthand' symbols. Discuss the selection of symbols and short cuts used to convey meaning and how we all have to agree if we wish to communicate with each other. Introduce or refer to recognized symbols and computer icons, and set up searches into symbols around the world, like those used by Aboriginal children in Australia.

Extend the invention to other practical, exploratory areas of the curriculum. How would the children represent or symbolize a forward roll? A mountain? A paint brush? A bang on the drum? An inquisitive person?

Practical enquiries and research

Suggestions for practical and research enquiries need to take account of new vocabulary and support children's access to this. Methods include:

- Constraints on the number of variables to focus on the key word/s (see Chapter 2). For example, putting objects with the same size, shape and nature in water, such as an apple, a pear and an orange (= float, sink, density).
- Clear evidence of the concept in question. For example, 'growth' can be illustrated by fast-growing objects such as mung beans, amaryllis or mould on bread in a sealed container.
- Using the same word/concept in a variety of contexts (see Chapter 4). For example, 'ball' can refer to a football, golf ball, ping-pong ball, airflow ball, squash ball and a marble, initiating investigations into rolling, floating, and so on.
- Using extreme examples of the same concept. For example, a heavy book and a pocketbook; a coconut and a strawberry seed.
- Displaying the new vocabulary before and/or after the enquiry on wall lists, mobiles or in class books. For example: rough, smooth, slippery; switch, battery, bulb, circuit, wire.

Stimulate practical and other enquiries by providing the starters for questions on cards, such as 'What is . . . ?'; 'Where is . . . ?' 'How many . . . ?'; 'Do all . . . ?' and asking children to complete them, for example: 'Do all horse-chestnut leaves have the same number of leaflets?' (see also Figure 5.2).

Classroom and school libraries need dictionaries which make definitions relevant and easy to read and books which enlighten and inform. Children need a focus for their enquiries. A questions box (Feasey and Thompson 1992) can activate enquiries with the questions chosen to suit the children's abilities and questions added by them too. For example:

- Can you find a picture of a butterfly? A dinosaur?
- Can you find out where cotton comes from?
- Can you find out who invented the electric light bulb?
- Can you find out which spiders are poisonous to human beings?

Apart from information books, there will always be related fiction and non-fiction to explore, inform and entertain – for example, grinding wheat into flour in *The Little Red Hen* (traditional). There are also nursery rhymes and songs which transmit information. Use the question box to encourage exploration and research here too:

- Can you find a rhyme about something we eat?
- Can you think of or find a song about winter?
- Can you find a story about a dog?

Children can use their research for other children by making notes about the sources of information they used. There could be a review notebook kept in the classroom where details of the book and the information it gives are recorded (Bradley 1996). This can also encourage children's critical and reflective skills and other children can comment too (see Figure 5.7).

Games to play
Quiz games can initiate and use children's researched information and help them to formulate questions. Children involved in such games will also discover the need to make decisions about acceptable and unacceptable answers. It takes great skill to devise questions that are both unambiguous and provide one-word answers (e.g. 'Trivial Pursuit', Standard Assessment Tasks).

Title	Author	Content	Comments	Location	Reader
The Amazing Voyage of the Cucumber Sandwich	Dr Peter Rowan	About digesting food in the body	Like a story – good and funny	School library	John
		Tells you about why we can't live on chips!	Great! I like the drawings		Amy

Figure 5.7 Example of a review notebook

Children can use new ideas and vocabulary to work as individuals or pairs on acrostics, rhyming words and poems. Children can use the outcomes of their enquiries to make 'find the words' squares. Townend *et al.* (1991) suggest excellent, cross-cultural ideas.

Play verbal or written versions of the game 'What is the question?' in which you provide the answers and the children devise a variety of questions to fit them. The complexity of the answers will depend on the age and experience of the children. For example:

- It's red.
- It's round on the top.
- At 7 o'clock tomorrow.
- It's probably plastic.
- Only if all the wires are joined up.
- Carbon dioxide, I think.

This game can also be played by drawing their 'answers' and asking for questions, any and all of which will be possible if the 'answers' are open-ended. The game will stimulate thought and curiosity in the children's minds.

School and parental support for the language of enquiry echoes that in previous chapters. We want children to come to school and go home with questions. Home and school are partners in supporting enquiries, whether communicated verbally or in writing. Sharing discoveries with the wider community will happen informally and in formal displays of work and assemblies. We are succeeding if the children go home with an enthusiasm to tell their families, 'Guess what I found out today!'

Assessment

1 Do the children ask a variety of questions?
2 Do the children suggest ways of following up the questions?
3 Do the children persevere with an enquiry using a variety of sources of information?
4 Do the children feel confident to talk about their discoveries to others?
5 Do the children explore ideas and the use of new vocabulary?
6 Do the children record discoveries in a way that explains things clearly?
7 Do the children offer critical opinions about books, ideas or the results of a practical activity?

Summary

This chapter has outlined the acquisition of language and how this influences children's cognitive development. Language is essential in enquiry-based learning, particularly speaking and listening. New and sometimes precise vocabulary and meaning can present a challenge to teachers and children in teaching and learning in the classroom. Enquiries can be supported by teachers using open-ended questions and providing practical activities and secondary sources of information. Ownership of the language helps children to understand and use words meaningfully. Shared communication gives children access to and practice in using a variety of language formats.

Questions to ask

1 What strategies do you use when introducing new or less familiar vocabulary?
2 Ask someone to observe you or tape record one or two of your discussions with the children: how frequently do you use open-ended questions?
3 When focusing on a new concept, how many different contexts do you use to illustrate or investigate the concept?
4 How can you vary the ways in which you ask children to record the results of their enquiries?
5 How can you increase the opportunities for classroom debates?

6

How to cross the river without getting wet: problem solving

Cameo 1

Four-year-old Richard is concerned when the home area is 'removed' from one corner of the classroom to the other. 'There's no clock now in the home corner,' he says, referring to the wall clock in the vacated space.

'You're right,' says the teacher. 'What can we do?'

'I know,' says Richard. He gets a wooden brick and using a circular shape and a felt-tip pen, draws a clock face with some numbers on one side. Delighted with this, he puts his clock into the new home area. Ten minutes later he returns despondently with his clock. 'It doesn't work,' he says.

'You're right,' says the teacher. 'Can you think of something?'

'I know,' says Richard. He goes away and comes back triumphantly. 'It works now,' he says, 'it's electric!' He shows the back of the brick where he has drawn a resemblance of a battery and a circuit.

Cameo 2

A Year 2 class are reporting back after a visit to a local park which has a stream.

Jennifer:	We tried to cross the river.
Teacher:	Did you?
Jennifer:	But we saw some stones but there was a high hill and we couldn't get over.
Teacher:	So how do you think it's best to cross the river?
Jennifer:	Bridge.
Teacher:	Or?

John:	Or you can cut the tree down and you can walk across the tree.
Julie:	But you gotta be careful, very careful.
Teacher:	Why?
Julie:	So, you could slip off.
Christine:	And the log might roll.
Teacher:	And the log might roll? So, Jennifer says the hill or the bank was too high. You could cross it by a bridge or a tree log. Are there any other ways of crossing the stream without getting your feet wet?
Tony-Anne:	You could tie a rope around a tree and swing across.
Teacher:	Good idea. What might happen to you if you didn't jump off in time?
Steven:	You might go back again.
Teacher:	You might go back again. Or?
Steven:	You might fall in the river. [general laughter]

The discussion leads to the creation of a blue crepe paper river across the classroom floor with various bridges made from construction kits, recycled materials, newspaper and so on.

Cameo 3

A Year 5 class are applying their knowledge of electricity in individual and group projects: making cranes with electromagnetic pickups, homes with burglar alarms and so on. Harry, Simon and Rohan have made a two-storey house with lights and a doorbell. Harry's 5-year-old sister Mary comes to see it. She plays with it then looks disappointed. 'The top light should go off when the bottom light goes on.'

'Yeah,' says Harry, 'but we can't do that.'

'We could try it tomorrow, if you like?' the teacher suggests.

The following day she asks the children to make two separate circuits from the same battery pack while she uses card, foil and a split pin to give them the starting point for a double switch. She leaves them with this, more pins and kitchen foil to explore and discuss their ideas and solutions. They come back later delighted with their success – it works – one light goes on when the other goes off. 'Great,' says the teacher, 'but how do you turn the light off?'

Quick as a flash Rohan moves the foil into the centre. 'There,' she says, 'that's off!'

Simon says thoughtfully, 'What about a triple switch . . . ?'

Introduction

How did the problems arise in these situations? Whose problems were they? What skills and knowledge did the children need to help them solve the problems? What evidence is there of creativity in the solutions? What responses did the teachers make in each case and why?

This chapter looks at problem solving as an innate and necessary process of learning, involving creativity and logical behaviour. Problem solving is an approach that is relevant to all areas of learning but has special significance in practical problem solving and in developing critical thinking skills. There is a wide variety of stimulating problems that can be initiated in the classroom and solved effectively, particularly when children are working in groups.

Problem solving as a cognitive process

An ability to solve problems is an indication of intelligence, like an orang-utan digging out termites with a stick. Human beings use a vast range of ideas and tools to solve problems and survive, work and enjoy life. We usually find solutions to most problems, on our own or with help from other people.

There are different types of problem solving: mechanistic and intellectual. We deal with physical problems at a level which does not require much thought – we get a cloth to mop up spilt milk, we break into a run when we see the bus coming. Intellectual problem solving is characterized by thinkers scanning the given information, their existing knowledge and their feelings about the problem and selecting an appropriate response from several options. We plan chess moves and weigh up the consequences of taking a new job or moving house. We 'put on our thinking caps', 'rack our brains' and sometimes 'sleep on it', hoping that our minds may somehow present us with *the* solution or alternative options.

We are solving problems most of the time, usually unconsciously. Taking the process 'for granted' can devalue the skills of problem solving. We need to be effective in finding and using information and theories, relevant both to school and life situations, and be aware of our own effectiveness: 'All children face problems but not all children achieve success in tackling them' (Fisher 1990: xii). We cannot solve problems without thinking.

Problem solving requires the thinker to perceive the wholeness of the problem as well as identify particular aspects of the problem. Finding solutions requires thinking of a variety of known responses or creating new ideas and trying these out in a series of logical steps. Ability to solve intellectual and practical problems is the basis for mature, adaptive thinking (Bruner 1966; de Bono 1970; McPeck 1981) and prepares children well to tackle the events and conflicts of everyday life.

Problem solving is closely related to creative thinking and reasoning but differs in that it involves the application of these as well as critical, reflective thought (McPeck 1981; Siegel 1988). Problem solving is a process at the end of which there is a product, whether a mental solution, a design or an artefact. 'The process of learning is as important as its content, since it often determines how much information and understanding is retained and the extent to which it can be applied in practice' (Paul Hamlyn Foundation 1993: 87).

Problem solving is a valuable approach to teaching and learning across the curriculum but of particular value in practical enquiries (Johnsey 1986). The process differs from more typically scientific thinking which is concerned with 'problem posing' (Harlen 1996). Science poses questions such as 'How far . . . ?' and 'What will happen if . . . ?' more often than 'How can we . . . ?' and 'Can we make something that will . . . ?'

Problem-solving situations encourage innovative, lateral thinking, like Richard's solutions to his 'working clock' in Cameo 1 and the children's ideas in Cameo 2. Practice in problem solving encourages skills, positive attitudes and active, rather than 'passive' knowledge (see Figure 6.1). Such skills and attitudes are transferable.

Enquiries using information technology present their own opportunities. Children learn how to:

- gather and organize information;
- store and manipulate data;
- 'locate and extract information from a variety of sources;
- record information in appropriate ways;
- draft and edit materials being prepared for presentation;
- give and receive information via IT' (Parkin 1991: 21);
- interact with software games and simulation programmes.

Learning opportunities	Skills
Learning relevant to children	Thinking logically and behaving systematically
Challenging and motivating	Thinking creatively and using materials imaginatively
Purposeful, first hand experience	Planning and investigative skills
Application of knowledge and experience	Identifying problems and devising solutions
Developing social skills	Finding ways to control aspects of our environment
Cross-curricular applications	Individual and cooperative interaction
Using language and maths skills purposefully	Ability to design and make
Using motor skills and developing coordination	Ability to evaluate and modify
Developing competence and self-regulation	Ability to reflect

Attitudes	Active knowledge
Development of self-confidence	Materials
Using initiative	Mechanisms
Curiosity and questioning	Systems
Critical thinking	Human behaviour, needs, interests
Patience	Forces and energy
Perseverance	Cause and effect
Tolerance and compromise	
Sensitivity	
Enthusiasm	

Figure 6.1 The range of children's learning when meeting and solving problems
Source: de Bóo 1987b; Fisher 1990; Ritchie 1995

What is the problem?

The starting point of an enquiry is the result of conflict or a challenge (Blenkin and Kelly 1981; Meadows 1983; Kahney 1986). A challenge confronts the learner with a question, their own or externally imposed: 'What makes you say that?', 'Do you think it would work if . . . ?' (Elstgeest 1985). All problems are set in a particular context although the surrounding factors are not always clearly identified. A problem is only perceived *as* a problem if some-one meets an obstacle that prevents them from reaching a goal.

Problems in real life are likely to be multi-faceted with several options, any one of which may present further problems. In these situations we learn to compromise and choose the 'best fit' for the circumstances. Many of the problems children meet in school are abstracted from reality, with one 'right answer'. While these can assess recall or test developing skills they do not usually extend the children's thinking (Fisher 1990). For example, prac-tising a forward roll reinforces motor skills and self-confidence. Asking children to find out how many different ways there are of rolling their bodies on the mat requires thought and will lead to exploration and self-testing. The skill of teaching is to ensure the right degree of challenge in the problems the children attempt to solve. All *cognitive* problems involve higher-level thinking skills (Norris 1992).

Whose problem is it?

Ownership of the problem influences which thinking skills are engaged and the nature of the problem can lead to greater or lesser levels of creative performance. Teachers who 'present' children with a specified problem elicit fewer and less varied responses (Tuma and Reif 1980). Where children identify or 'dis-cover' their own problem, they give more and varied responses. In order to develop problem-posing or problem-solving skills, children need opportunities to investigate and question their *own* environment (Harlen 1996); children who solve their own prob-lems have a greater sense of achievement.

Development of children's skills

Children are predisposed to solve problems; the toddler is deter-mined to crawl towards the toy, children turn a stick into a sword or an umbrella. This requires and fosters determination, per-severance, ingenuity and imagination.

Young children attempt to solve problems using existing *simple* theories. These develop into more complex generalized theories (DeLoache and Brown 1987). The development may occur in three phases: procedural, metaprocedural and conceptual (Russell 1993):

- *Procedural phase*: children's responses to the problem are rarely planned and are governed by positive and negative feedback or information (Cameo 1); children try a variety of solutions in a non-systematic way.
- *Metaprocedural phase*: children's responses are increasingly governed by their own ideas or internal modelling, and less by external stimuli (Cameo 2).
- *Conceptual phase*: children's internal modelling of the problem and theoretical understanding allows them to think through and reject unsatisfactory solutions. This reduces wasted effort and increases competence (see Chapter 3).

Success in problem solving motivates positive developmental change (Karmiloff-Smith 1984), and this has implications for classroom teaching.

Problematic situations

Children do not appear to have difficulty in adopting a problem-solving approach but problem *situations* can pose difficulties:

- Limited opportunities and few challenges can restrict development.
- Challenges that are too many or too great may cause loss of confidence.
- Background knowledge is needed, and the greater this is, the greater the success in finding solutions. 'Good problem solvers know more than less successful problem solvers' (Fisher 1990: 114). Furthermore, good problem solvers have understood some of the knowledge they have acquired.
- Language skills are needed. Children who are able to ask questions, ask others for ideas and support or conduct searches in books or software find effective solutions more easily.
- Problems in practical settings require motor skills and expertise with tools.

Complexity, fear of failure and repetition of erroneous actions can damage children's self-esteem and discourage the development of confidence in problem solving. Success increases children's ability to face new challenges. In Cameo 3, the teacher ensured that the children had the resources to succeed.

Children addressing and solving problems, whether presented or discovered, need:

- support for their curiosity;
- help in understanding the problem;
- approval for an ingenious or straightforward solution to the problem.

Although the zone of proximal development (Vygotsky 1986) varies from individual to individual, I have seen 5-year-old children, with support, solve problems designed for 7–8-year-old pupils.

The teacher's role

Attitudes

Many primary teachers lack confidence in their own ability to teach practical subjects such as science and design and technology which involve children in practical problem solving (SCAA 1994; Siraj-Blatchford 1995). However, the same teachers show considerable expertise as problem solvers in the classroom, managing an effective environment for teaching and learning. Class teachers face problems on a daily basis – juggling time, resources, differentiated learning objectives, children's moods and needs, interruptions to lessons and the impact of weather, visitors and rehearsals. Given training in the use of, for example, tools, materials, mechanisms and strategies, teachers feel more confident to increase the children's opportunities for practical problem solving. Teachers work best with a new method when they have integrated it into their educational ideology and their personality (*Hadow Report* 1931).

Because problem situations can be difficult to pitch at exactly the right level for all children, an atmosphere of trust and positive personal relationships is needed between the teacher and the children. Children need to feel that 'I can think this out for myself', like the children in the cameos.

Planning appropriate activities

Setting the context for problem-solving enquiries embraces more than organizing the physical provision of the classroom. The starting point may come from teachers or children (see Figure 6.2). We cannot always rely on children to identify viable problems for themselves which also encompass teachers' current educational

Figure 6.2 Larry's old clock is reassembled.

priorities. However, using appropriate stimuli (see the discussion on classroom context in the next section), teachers can set the scene for children to 'discover' or address problems which meet learning objectives yet leave enough flexibility for children's self-motivated enquiries (Kimbell *et al.* 1991).

Interdisciplinary topic-based enquiries are vehicles which can capitalize on children's interests but may sometimes lead to confusion. It is possible to lose sight of the greater learning objectives in enthusiasm for focused activities on a theme (Blenkin and Kelly 1981). It is equally possible in the current educational climate, in which concepts and skills are frequently abstracted from real contexts, to lose sight of the fact that children learn in an eclectic, holistic way (Paul Hamlyn Foundation 1993).

Figure 6.3 6-year-old Hilary wrote (original spellings): 'I maed a car. It was easy to make the boddy. But the weels got stuk and wudt go roud.'

Whatever the origin of the enquiry, teachers need to evaluate the learning potential of the situation regarding:

- the relevance to the children;
- the skills and knowledge required;
- the possible obstacles;
- the educational goals.

Planning can then be carried out with the children to reinforce effective systems of behaviour.

Open-ended questions such as 'What might happen if . . . ?' and 'How can we . . . ?' will encourage investigating and testing, designing and making. 'Do you want to change anything?' and 'Did you have any difficulties? What did you do?' will encourage children's evaluative, critical thinking (Ritchie 1995) (see Figure 6.3). Other problems can be set for thinking and debate.

The term 'designing' needs to be wide enough to include:

Ways of working: a child's annotated drawing

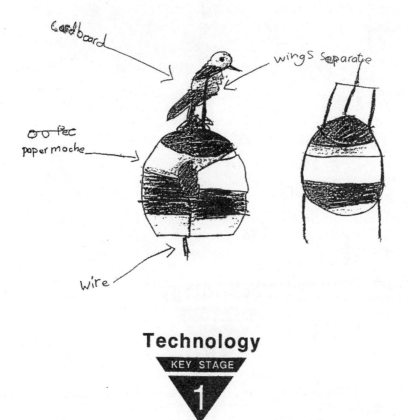

Figure 6.4 Johnny designs a helmet with a parrot

- draft drawings of children's intentions (see Figure 6.4);
- mental modelling;
- verbalizing ideas in advance or instead of action (Siraj-Blatchford 1995).

Visualizing their design reinforces children's thinking and planning skills and explores prior experience in a purposeful way (de Bono 1970). Younger children do not spontaneously use drawings to help them present their design ideas but many of them

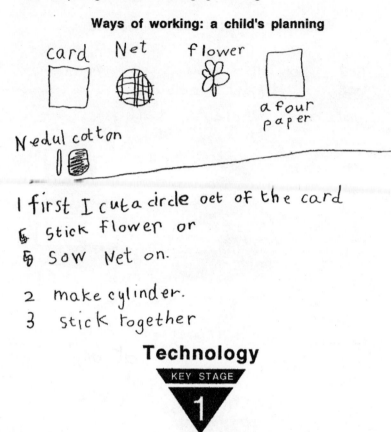

Ways of working: a child's planning

card   Net   flower

Nedul cotton

I first I cut a circle oet of the card
& Stick flower or
& Sow Net on.

2 make cylinder.
3 stick together

a four
paper

Technology

KEY STAGE

1

Figure 6.5 Sally-Ann plans to make a hat to wear in the school parade (Year 1)

will respond well to the idea on occasions, given time and support (see Figure 6.5). Increasingly, designs come to mean written plans and reflections (see Figure 6.6), diagrams, lists of materials and prototypes which should be an exploratory exercise free of the possibility of failure (Ritchie 1995). A period of planning time allows the teacher to anticipate possible obstacles to success in advance and influence the direction of early modifications.

It is fundamentally important to keep the challenges simple at first. Success truly does breed success. Too much complexity too soon can lead to disappointment and a loss of self-esteem. This can deter children from further participation.

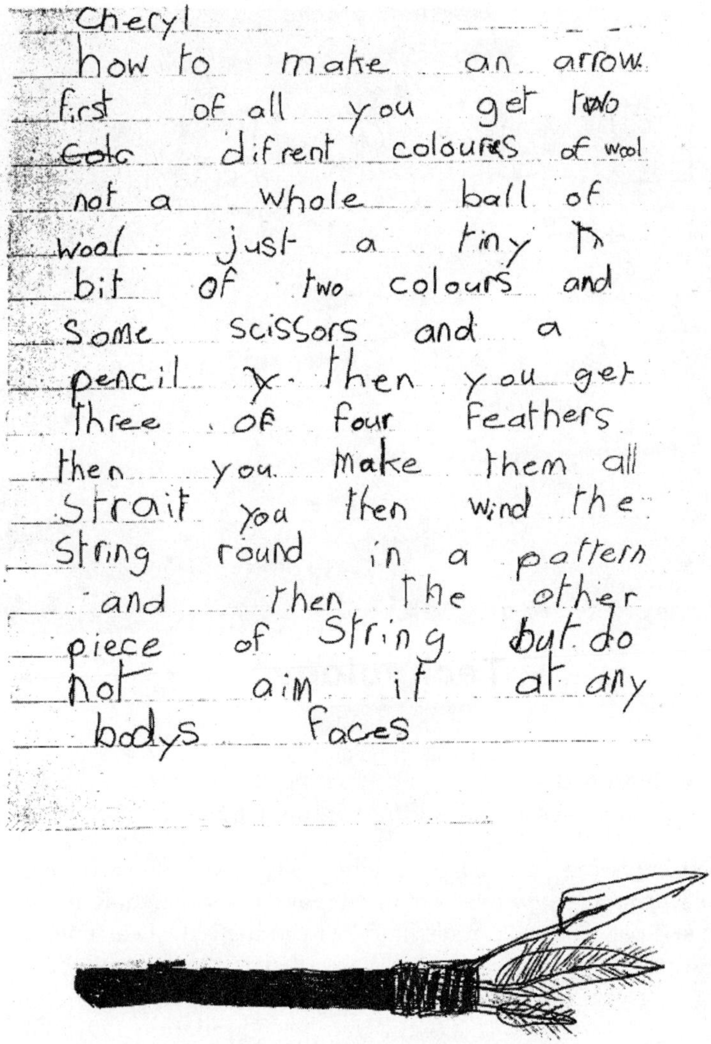

> Cheryl
> how to make an arrow
> first of all you get two
> colo difrent coloures of wool
> not a whole ball of
> wool just a tiny th
> bit of two colours and
> some scissors and a
> pencil x then you get
> three or four feathers
> then you make them all
> strait you then wind the
> string round in a pattern
> and then the other
> piece of string but do
> not aim if at any
> bodys faces

Figure 6.6   Cheryl instructs her friends on how to make an arrow (Year 2)

Teaching styles and group work

Primary teachers who use a range of teaching styles tend to stimulate the children's capacity to learn independently and work col-
laboratively, although there is some pressure currently to use

Figure 6.7 Alan video-filming his friends

tightly controlled situations and teaching styles. Finding the right balance is a professional skill (see Figure 6.8):

> Concentrating on fixed-pace, whole class teaching can leave the learning requirements of many pupils unsatisfied. Relying on self-paced work can result in low productivity. Learning in groups can be more effective than either of these if members of the group have the right 'mix' of ideas and approaches.
>
> (Paul Hamlyn Foundation 1993: 88)

Even where children are working alone they may need to consult and share with others. Alan (Figure 6.7) made a video to 'photograph his friends':

> Children working in pairs and groups produce more effective solutions to logical problems than children working alone. The social process of discussion and argument acts as a catalyst to thinking. The opportunity to suggest, reject and spark

Figure 6.8   Children collaborate to make a monster with eyes that light up

off new ideas helps to synthesise and consolidate a child's thinking.

(Fisher 1990: 137)

In appropriate group settings, children behave more like competent, intelligent social operators than when left to address problems in isolation (Bruner and Haste 1987). Dealing with challenges demands perseverance, concentration and decision making; group collaboration teaches assertiveness and compromise.

The amount of time that children spend working alone with the computer may increase in the future. Problem solving with other children in the classroom may become increasingly important in children's social training.

Intervention

Intervention may not always be necessary. Giving the children opportunities to think of their own solutions may be the first step (Cameo 1). As soon as the teacher does intervene, the nature and direction of the child's enquiry changes (Cameo 3). Intervention is advisable in some situations, as follows:

Lack of confidence
Sometimes the size and scale of the problem may not be matched to the children's levels of knowledge and skills. Children can become anxious and confused as to what is expected of them. The original goal can be adapted or broken down into manageable aspects, with delegated tasks, straightforward instructions and, where necessary, active participation offered in solving a few of the problems.

Over-ambition
Children are not always aware of their abilities and skills and set themselves over-ambitious, non-viable targets. Mismatched challenges can cause disappointment. If children's plans seem complicated, we can persuade them to simplify them 'to begin with' and elaborate them later, or say 'Try it – but we may not have enough resources to do it exactly the way you've planned'. When all else fails, children can learn to accept disappointments, as long as they have more successes.

Lack of resources
Children and teachers do not always have enough resources and training for practical problem solving and investigational or intellectual enquiries. Children can be pragmatic and realistic if given the opportunity: regular discussions can identify materials or sources of information to bring or borrow from home, local secondary schools or teachers' centres; some materials, equipment and publications may need listing for future purchasing.

Distraction
Children can forget the original problem to be solved and follow up other problems or go down blind alleys. Questions help to focus children's attention on particular aspects of the problem. Children may need reminding of the overall problem they are trying to solve. Tools and materials can be checked and minor obstacles identified to be solved by the teacher. Children will need positive comments on how much has been achieved so far.

Figure 6.9 Humpty Dumpty before the fall!

Time needed
Children underestimate the amount of time needed for an activity. Teachers, too, often underestimate the amount of time needed to train children in the use of new equipment or for interim discussions on the progress of the work, problems met and tackled, and modifications evaluated (Driver 1983).

Dealing with the unexpected
We all know that the best laid plans may go astray as, for example, when Humpty Dumpty wouldn't balance on the 'wall' (see Figure 6.9). There can be no preparation other than that needed for every teaching day – flexibility, ingenuity, sharing

ideas and errors with the children in an appropriate way, and being ready to learn from the occasional flop!

Feedback: teacher to children, children to children

Feedback to the children can help them to become aware of their skills by articulating their successes, for example: 'You all had some great ideas – you won't be able to use them all but some will definitely work!'; 'You planned that very well!'; 'You solved the problem, then?'; 'I see you've modified the winding mechanism – didn't the other one work?'

Asking questions will encourage children to evaluate their process and product:

- What have you learnt from this?
- Is there anything else you want to find out about?
- Would you do anything differently next time?

Young children need practice in organizing and selecting relevant information for reporting back. Opportunities to report back develop analytical and language skills and self-esteem. Teachers can help children to plan the process and present information by suggesting structures and asking questions. This can be done verbally on an individual or group basis, written on 'consulting cards' or in an information technology programme folder:

Plan	*Report*
What are you trying to do or find out?	We were trying to . . .
What problems might you meet?	We had a few problems . . .
Can you think of different ways to solve these?	We tried to solve them by . . .
Do you have the resources you need?	We succeeded when we . . .
Do you need to learn how to use tools or equipment?	We are most proud of . . .
Is there anyone who can help you?	
How much time will you need?	We have finished our report.
How will you present your product?	Would you like to ask us any questions?

Inviting the rest of the children to ask questions will show interest and identify areas of confusion which itself feeds back to the reporting group.

Feedback does not always have to take the form of prosaic description. Encourage children to write about their problems – poems, limericks, jokes, and fantastical stories (see Chapter 5).

Equality of opportunity in practical problem solving

Boys seem to assume that they are capable of solving problems. Girls are perfectly capable but they can lose confidence fairly easily and leave the task uncompleted (Siraj-Blatchford 1991). However, 'girls can perform well in investigational work and problem solving if the groups are sensitively organized and the problems are not dominated by traditional male-role life situations' (Parkin 1991: 52). For example, given free choice, boys tend to dominate the use of constructional kits which help them develop their spatial awareness. Programming to include regular use by girls and extending time constraints can give an impetus to girls' spatial development.

Girls and boys show interest in different foci, social contexts (girls) and vehicles (boys) (Harding 1983). Analysing the relevance of the problem to boys and girls, providing problems or tasks which value different interests and varying the tasks on a regular basis can give equality of opportunity. This strategy can increase awareness of other community groups too. For example, everyone could be asked to design and sometimes make:

- a house with a balcony;
- a car pulling a caravan;
- a garden;
- a fairground;
- a wheelchair for a doll (Key Stage 2 children could borrow dolls from Nursery or Reception classes);
- a model of a walking frame for a baby or a senior citizen.

Such efforts can be effective: 'Positive discrimination in favour of girls can increase their interest and confidence in constructional play with no detrimental effect upon boys' (Parkin 1991: 63). Setting problems in this way will trigger children's observation of real objects and research for more information.

The classroom context for problem solving

The primary classroom is alive with the potential for practical and intellectual problems. Solutions will vary: children may acquire knowledge or information, change their opinions, dramatize a concept, design a product, make a game or a three-dimensional model, use information technology for a purpose. One of the best outcomes of such an exercise, from the teacher's point of view, is not only seeing the enthusiasm with which children tackle the problem but using the result as evidence of children's developing skills and *understanding*. Understanding, as discussed in Chapter 4, is not always easy to assess but children's responses to a challenge can reveal it.

Stimuli and starting points

The stimuli and starting points for children's problem solving suggested below address many areas of children's learning. Some of the ideas would initiate 'stand-alone' designs, like the egg-cracking machine (see Figure 6.10) which states: 'The tea pot tips up. It fills the beaker. The rocking chair tips backwards, undoes the string. This knocks this off this'. Other ideas would inspire debates or long-term projects. Levels of difficulty would relate to the age and experience of the children, as younger children use fewer tools and mechanisms, for example:

- Year R: make a vehicle without a moving mechanism; Year 4: use wheels and axles.
- Year 2: obtain movement using string and elastic; Year 5: use these and levers, pulleys and pneumatic tubing.
- Year 1: need tabletop stability provided; Year 4: make their models free-standing.

In all open-ended challenges, it will be necessary to prescribe certain conditions, such as time allowance and resources to be used. The focus will determine some of the restrictions. Limiting the choice of materials focuses attention on properties of the available materials and fitness for purpose. Limitations on size focuses attention on scale and measurement.

Figure 6.10 The egg-cracking machine

Ideas for challenges

Phenomena

Specific problems set by the teacher provide a conceptual focus and reveal children's understanding of the concepts. Ask the children to design and/or make:

- A (free-standing) plant from planet Curio that makes a sound to attract insects whenever the wind (hairdrier) blows. Areas of learning: Sound (making and travelling), plants and seed propagation, different climatic zones.
- A mechanism that will water the plant(s) every day while the family are on holiday for a week. Areas of learning: living things, materials, water, forces and their effects, time, mechanisms.
- A fabric tester that will 'wear out' different fabrics into holes. Ideas about materials, forces, friction, mechanisms.
- A ping-pong ball machine for the school fête that aims to drop balls into a bucket placed at a distance. Ideas about forces, stored energy, measurement, control.
- A grocery box theatre for puppets, with a curtain that will move up or aside and stage lights that can dim or brighten. Ideas about forces and movement, electricity and dimmer switches.

Ideas can be represented in three-dimensional models, in mime, or collages with children having freedom to interpret the concept, for example:

Darkness	Wheels
Not safe to eat	Water
Melting	Weather changes
Predators	Rock formation
Our solar system	Electricity
Noise and music	Trees
Colour	Machines
Bees	Buildings
Life cycles	Animals who like to hide
Reflections	

Stories

Some of the children's favourite stories or nursery rhymes can act as inspirations for posing problems. Can the children:

- Make a Humpty Dumpty and a wall for him to sit on?
- Make a Hickory Dickory clock with a mouse that goes up the clock?
- Make different houses for the Three Little Pigs: one which will blow down easily, one which will blow down less easily, one which won't blow down?
- Make a chair for Goldilocks that will be stable for a little teddy bear but collapse under the weight of a heavier doll (older children)?
- Suggest reasons why the Big Bad Wolf always loses (*Little Red Riding Hood, The Three Little Pigs, Peter and the Wolf*)? Is it fair to wolves?

Classroom story books can be analysed for potential for enquiries and problems that could lead to knowledge and understanding, thoughtful debate and design/make opportunities – that is, does the book:

- Inspire a research enquiry?
- Inspire discussion?
- Suggest ideas for modelling (draw, design and make, mime)?

For example, the story *Elmer* (McKee 1980) could lead to:

Enquiries into	*Discussions about*	*Ideas for 3-D models*
Elephants	Differences between	Sad and happy moods
Colours	people (language,	Changing colour
Camouflage	families, skin colour)	An elephant with a moving part
		A patchwork hat/coat

While *The Secret Garden* (Hodgson-Burnett 1911) might lead to:

Enquiries into	*Discussions about*	*Ideas for 3-D models*
Growth, seasons	People who are	Something coming
Robins, decay	lonely or grieving	back to life
	Gardens that are	Recovering from
	neglected	illness
	Seasonal effects on	An indoor or outdoor
	our feelings	garden
		A small garden using modelling clay
		A pop-up robin
		A seasonal dice game

Use information books also, to challenge and inspire, for example *The Do-It-Yourself House that Jack Built* (Yeoman and Blake 1994).

Events
Use calendar and school events to initiate problem-solving activities:

- Birthdays: how many biscuits can be made from the cake mix, or can you make 30 biscuits from the cake mix with none left over?
- Diwali: can you make a safe candle holder using . . . ?
- Christmas: can you make a halo light over baby Jesus' head in the crib?

Ask the children how many design ideas can come from Mr Jones' class outing: 'Mr Jones' class went in the coach to the safari park. They had packed lunches, safety boxes and the adults had brochures and maps with them. The children looked at all the animals, had rides on the park buggies and went in the playground before they bought souvenirs and came back to school'.

There is potential here for designing and making the following: the coaches, packed lunches, lunch boxes, safety boxes, safety contents, brochures and maps; letters to parents and the safari park; the animals and their enclosures; a map of the safari park; the park buggies, the playground games, the souvenirs, and models of children and adults. There is also potential for debating the nature of animals kept in captivity, preserving species, and people's perception of the children when visiting out-of-school venues.

Set challenges
Some of these will arise from areas of study planned in the classroom but some can stand alone, adapted to the abilities and interests of the children. For example, can the children design and/or make:

- A (free-standing) bridge made out of newspaper that has a 1 m span and can support a toy car or a 1kg mass?
- A folding chair for one of the dolls?
- A marble run from the table to the floor that will last: as long as possible? 5 seconds?
- A remote control egg-cracking machine (see Figure 6.10)?

- A dinosaur trap that lets you know when the dinosaur is caught?
- A head that can open its mouth (a person, crocodile or fish)
- A poster reminding children to be safe at the beach?
- A firefly whose tail lights up?
- A modelling-clay model of a woodlouse, spider, worm or snail?
- A stimulating trail around the school?

Disassembling or 'how does it work?'
Ask the children to explore and explain the working of:

A paper clip	A wind-up toy
A bulldog clip	A bicycle
A felt-tip pen	A soft drinks carton and straw
Scissors	Armbands for swimming
A deck-chair	The classroom door
An egg whisk	

Consider setting up or participating in a class or school Challenge Day. If a school affair, invite parents and members of the local community to join you. The ingenuity and skills shown can delight the visitors and show how much work is involved and how much learning occurs. Year 2 and Year 6 children showed their originality and evaluation skills as young designers when they made puppets with moving parts:

'We've given it eyes on stalks – that go in and out like a gnome. You know how a gnome looks at you!'
'His tongue pokes in and out. It looks like our teacher, Mr G—'
[giggle]
'He can look upwards when the fly lands on his nose, but we can't do the fly yet.'
'He has got a body but we haven't got time to give him any legs so he's a legless robot!'

(de Bóo 1987b)

Fault-finding or 'what's wrong?'
Can the children sort out the following:

- A (safe) kitchen mixture where the foods got mixed up (say, icing sugar, dried peas, broad beans, rice)?

- A (safe) beach mixture of say, rounded pebbles, sand, salt crystals and milk bottle tops?
- A mixture of water and vegetable oil?
- Simple electricity sets that might have a (safe) faulty bulb, battery, switch, wire?

Systems
Can the children suggest ways to improve:

- How long it takes the classes to assemble in the hall?
- The time it takes to get ready for PE so no time is lost?
- Ways to let parents know when there is some special work they ought to come and see?
- Ways that everyone gets to play in the open space in the playground?

Can the children suggest things in the school or class system that could be improved?

Games
Can the children design and/or make a toy or game:

- For babies?
- For people who can't hear very well?
- To test children's reflexes?
- That uses magnetism?
- That uses electricity?
- That uses dice?

Information technology

Children are not often daunted by problems encountered on the computer although they can get frustrated sometimes. Apart from data-handling and recording work, there are software programs which are designed to set children problems with achievable solutions, such as: *My First Incredible Dictionary; Our Facts; Creepy Crawlies; The Lost Frog; The Way Things Work;* and *The Ultimate Human Body* (details in Bibliography).

If the computer is used to word-process handwritten stories, make sure it is not simply used as a typewriter. Give children challenges to edit, cut and paste, present the work as for a book, a newspaper or a children's magazine. Encourage the use of fonts and illustrations in layout and printing.

The expanding potential for enquiries and communication via the computer opens up the children's world from school to school (electronic mailboxes) and worldwide (the Internet). Such linked enquiries are important for isolated schools and exciting for schools in different regions (country and urban studies of traffic); in different climates (schools in the Scottish Highlands and on the Cornish coast); and in different countries (England, France, Australia). E-mail and computer conferencing can support:

- teachers' enquiries;
- searches for knowledge and information;
- ideas for activities to teach certain concepts;
- awareness of useful resources and the discussion of issues and possible solutions (Davis and Keast 1991).

Resources, training and safety

Readers are referred to the discussion in Chapter 2 on training and safety in the use of tools, such as craft knives, cutting boards and glue guns. The principal point is that training is necessary *before* the project begins.

Assessment

1 Do the children identify and articulate problems encountered?
2 Do the children offer possible solutions to problems? Alternative solutions?
3 Do the children reflect on the proposed solutions, evaluating their effectiveness?
4 Do the children cooperate well with other children? Adults?
5 Are the children confident in using tools and equipment purposefully and safely?
6 Are the children confident in presenting work to others?

Summary

Solving intellectual and practical problems challenges children's thinking and coordination. Finding solutions develops logical and creative thinking, and children's confidence in their ability to solve problems is transferred to other situations. Their motor and social skills develop in cooperative projects. Children need support in defining and tackling their own problems and success is influential in the growth of self-esteem. Practical problem solving plays a role throughout the curriculum and teachers can encourage this by providing opportunities and resources. A safe, effective environment for pursuing enquiries helps children to understand and accept constraints and compromise.

Questions to ask

1 How can you create more opportunities for children to initiate or respond to problem-solving challenges?
2 How can you establish an environment in which children are aware that they are solving problems?
3 How can you improve the resources that will initiate and support practical problem solving?
4 How often do you meet, and solve, problems in the classroom (minor or major, practical and intellectual)?
5 How could you set up a special Problem Solving Challenge event for your class or the whole school on a termly basis?

7

Conclusion

Introduction

The following case study shows how children were encouraged to explore, classify, solve problems, plan, investigate and communicate what they found out. Enquiries were initiated by the teacher's challenging questions.

Initiating the enquiry

A parent came into her Year 2 daughter's class to offer a large piece of beige, fake-fur fabric. 'Can you use this?' she asked, 'it's left over from work – they were going to throw it away.'

The teacher chose to make immediate use of the gift although that meant reorganizing scheduled activities to incorporate the fake-fur fabric while retaining her current learning objectives.

Exploring, classifying, planning, researching

Later that day, the teacher gave the fabric to the children to explore. 'What can you tell me about this?' she asked, and 'what does it remind you of? What can we make with it?' The children felt and smelt the fabric, pulled and ruffled it and suggested teddy bears, guinea pigs, fur hats and rats. The rats idea brought a chorus of shivers and 'yuk's' and provoked discussion about fears of rats and other animals. Eventually, the class voted to make rats and searched for information books, pictures, stories and poems about rats, like *The Pied Piper of Hamelin* (Robert Browning, traditional).

The teacher chose to focus on the children's sewing skills, so she designed a template in a modified figure 8, and by laying the template alternately along the cloth, cut out 36 shapes.

Problem solving

Practical problems

Children folded the shapes inside out, sewed them up and stuffed them with tights. They selected and cut out cloth eyes and long string tails. The whiskers presented problems. Children suggested pipe cleaners (rejected as too heavy), thin wire (too sharp) and compromised on thick cotton whiskers threaded through the noses. This worked and the children were all delighted with their rats (see Figure 7.1).

Mental challenges

Then Jason approached the teacher. 'My rat strokes the wrong way,' he said.

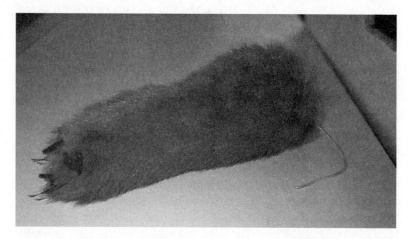

Figure 7.1 Mary's rat who likes to be stroked the 'wrong' way!

The teacher looked at the rat. It was true. Her heart sank. Within minutes it was quite clear that half the class had rats with fur that 'stroked the wrong way' having been cut *against* the pile of the fabric. The teacher had to rescue a potentially unhappy situation. 'What makes you think that?' she said.

Thinking and investigating

Jason stopped to think, then he and the others began to explain that *their* pets grew fur or hair from nose to tail rather than the other way round. 'What would happen if it didn't grow that way?' said the teacher.

Sally said, 'The rats might get stuck in the holes when their fur sticks up.'

Everyone laughed. 'What about us humans?' said the teacher. Discussion and investigation followed as the children talked, asked about and explored the direction that their own and their friends' hair grew. When the children went home, they were ready to test their theories about their family pets, including goldfish scales (yes, they too grow from nose to tail).

Gaining knowledge and communicating

Over the following weeks, time was created for:

- counting and making graphs of home pets, drawn by hand and generated on the computer;
- arguing the case for 'killing all rats' – the final vote was *not* unanimous;
- arguing the case for not keeping any animals in captivity, including pets;
- a visit from the RSPCA on caring for animals at home and in the wild;
- reading stories and poems, including *The Pied Piper* and *The Cat Who Wanted to Go Home* (Tomlinson 1991);
- writing versions of *The Pied Piper* and other poems about rats;
- drawing pictures of rats, the children's favourite animals and their pets;
- making question and answer cards using simple electricity kits that lit a bulb when the correct answer was given.

Figure 7.2   And out of the houses the rats came tumbling

Finally, *The Pied Piper* was dramatized and shown to the school and parents in sharing assembly, and the rats were displayed, quite horrifyingly, tumbling over bricks and out of boxes in the school foyer (see Figure 7.2).

The teacher had challenged the children's thinking and by following up their enquiries the children had acquired skills and knowledge and reflected on their attitudes and opinions. Their enthusiasm was unabated by the end of term and the teacher had considerable evidence for assessing their learning and evaluating the success of the project.

Appendix: basic resources for science enquiries

B = borrow; C = collect; M = make; P = purchase

A

Aeroplanes (safe toys)	P
Aluminium/kitchen foil	P
Aquarium/water tanks	P

B

Balloons	P
Balls, various	C/P
Batteries	P
Beans, dried	P
Bells, bicycle and other	P
Bicycle (occasionally)	B
Binoculars	B
Bird table	P
Blotting paper	P
Bubble solution	M
Building/construction toys/kits	P
Building/construction materials	P
Bulbs and bulb holders	P
Buzzers, electric	P

C

Camera	B
Candles	P
Cars (toys)	C/P
Clocks	C/P
Coal/charcoal	C/P
Colour paddles and acetates	P
Coloured materials	C
Cotton reels	C/P
Cotton thread/string	C/P
Cotton wool	P
Crocodile clips	P

D

Dolls, small and large	C/P

E

Electricity kits	P
Eye-droppers/pipettes	P

F

Fabrics	C
Fans	C
Feathers	C
Filter/coffee papers	P
Floaters and sinkers	C
Flower press	P
Food, fresh and dried	P
Fossils	C/P
Funnels	P

G

Gear wheels (DIY and commercial)	M/P
Guttering (for rolling and boats)	P
Gyroscope	P

H

Hair dryer	P
Herbs (indoor garden)	M/P
Hooks (s-shaped) for weighing	P
Horn (old car horn)	B
Hot air balloon	M
Household ingredients (e.g. vinegar, salt, flour, sugar, cornflour)	C/P

I

Inks	P
Insect boxes	M/P
Insect viewers	P

J

Jars (plastic; and glass if policy allows)	C/P
Jelly moulds	B/P

K

Kaleidoscope	B/P

L

Lenses	P
Litmus/universal indicator	P

M

Magnets (various)	P
Maps	C
Matches (kept safely)	P
Materials (various)	C
Measuring equipment	P
Measuring jars	P
Mechanical toys	B/P
Metals (various)	C/P
Microscopes	P
Mini-beasts (dead: safe) and alive (temporary)	C
Mirrors	P
Motors (electricity kits)	P
Musical instruments	C/P

N

Nails (various)	P
Nesting box	M
Nylon twine (anglers')	P

P

Pendulums	M
Petri dishes or other	P
Plaster of Paris	P
Pooters	P
Pots (various)	C
Prisms	P
'Problem posers' and 'prediction-inspirers'	M
Pulleys	P

R

Ramps	M
Recycled materials	C
Rocks collection	C/P
Rubber/plastic tubing	P

S

Salt	P
Sand	P
Sand/glasspaper	P
Sandtimers	P
Saucepans	P
Seed sprouters	M/P
Seeds	P
Seedtrays	M/P
Shells	C/P
Skeleton (plastic or facsimile)	P
Soaps	P
Soils (safe/fresh)	C
Springs	C/P
Squeezy bottles	C
Stethoscope (real or toy)	B

Straws	P	**W**	
Stroboscope	M/P	Washing powders (safe)	P
Suction pad/plunger	P	Water clocks	M
Switches	P	Water tanks	P
Syringes (plastic)	P	Water wheels	M/P
		Wind gauge	M/P
T		Wires	P
Thermometers (various)	P	Wood (safe)	C/P
Tools (gardening)	P	Woodwork tools	P
Toys + moving parts	P	Wormery	M/P
Tubing (plastic)	P		
Tuning forks	P	**Y**	
		Yogurt pots (and such)	C
V			
Vegetable oil	P		
Viewers (various)	P		

Bibliography

Allen, J.P.B. and Van Buren, P. (1971) *Noam Chomsky: Selected Readings*. London: Oxford University Press.

Asimov, I. (1984) *Asimov's New Guide to Science: A Revised Edition*. Harmondsworth: Penguin.

Association for Science Education (ASE) (1996) *Be Safe*. Hatfield: ASE.

Ausubel, D. (1968) *Educational Psychology: A Cognitive View*. New York: Holt, Rinehart & Winston.

Barnes, D. (1976) *From Communication to Curriculum*. Harmondsworth: Penguin.

Barnes, D., Britton, J. and Torbe, M. (1986) *Language, the Learner and the School*, 3rd edn. Harmondsworth: Penguin.

Baron, J. (1985) *Rationality and Intelligence*. New York: Cambridge University Press.

Bernstein, B. (1971) *Class, Codes and Control*. London: Routledge.

Black, P.J. and Lucas, A.M. (eds) (1993) *Children's Informal Ideas in Science*. London: Routledge.

Blenkin, G.M. and Kelly, A.V. (1981) *The Primary Curriculum*. London: Harper & Row.

Bradley, L.S. (1996) *Children Learning Science*. Oxford: Nash Pollock Publishing.

Brooker, L. (1996) Why do children go to school? Consulting children in the Reception class. *TACTYC*, 17 (1): 12–16.

Browne, N. (ed.) (1991) *Science and Technology in the Early Years*. Buckingham: Open University Press.

Bruner, J.S. (1966) *The Process of Education*. Cambridge, MA: Harvard University Press.

Bruner, J.S. (1968) *Processes of Cognitive Growth: Infancy*. Worcester, MA: Clark University Press.

Bruner, J.S. (1971) *The Relevance of Education*. New York: W.W. Norton & Co.

Bruner, J.S. and Haste, H. (1987) *Making Sense: The Child's Construction of the World*. London: Methuen.

Bruner, J.S., Goodnow, J.J. and Austin, G.A. (1956) *A Study of Thinking*. New York: Wiley.

Bruner, J.S., Olver, R.R. and Greenfield, P.M. (1966) *Studies in Cognitive Growth*. New York: Wiley.

Bruner, J.S., Jolly, A. and Sylva, K. (eds) (1976) *Play: Its Role in Evolution and Development*. Harmondsworth: Penguin.

Carey, S. (1985) *Conceptual Change in Childhood*. Cambridge, MA: MIT Press.

Carle, E. (1970) *The Very Hungry Caterpillar*. London: Picture Puffin.

Chomsky, N. quoted in Allen, J.P.B. and Van Buren, P. (1971) *Noam Chomsky: Selected Readings*. London: Oxford University Press.

Chomsky, N. (1976) *Reflections on Language*. London: Temple Smith.

Chomsky, N. (1980) *Rules and Representations*. Oxford: Basil Blackwell.

Claxton, G.L. (1991) *Educating the Enquiring Mind: The Challenge for Science Education*. Hemel Hempstead: Harvester Wheatsheaf.

Claxton, G.L. (1993a) Mini-theories: a preliminary model for learning science, in P.J. Black and A.M. Lucas (eds) *Children's Informal Ideas in Science*. London: Routledge.

Claxton, G.L. (1993b) The interplay of values and research in science education, in P.J. Black and A.M. Lucas (eds) *Children's Informal Ideas in Science*. London: Routledge.

CLIS (1987) *Children's Learning in Science Project*. Leeds: Centre for Studies in Science and Mathematics Education, University of Leeds.

Cosgrove, M. and Osborne, R. (1985) Lesson frameworks changing children's ideas, in R. Osborne and P. Freyberg (eds) *Learning in Science: The Implications of Children's Learning*. Auckland, NZ: Heinemann.

Counting Pictures (1994) Powys: Black Cat Educational Software.

Creepy Crawlies (1992) London: Media Design Interactive.

Davis, N. and Keast, D. (1991) Electronic communication between small schools. *Microscope*, 32: 28–30.

de Bono, E. (1970) *Lateral Thinking*. London: Ward Lock.

de Bóo, M. (1987a) Who killed the cat? *Primary Science Review*, 3: 16–18.

de Bóo, M. (1987b) The day of the young designers. *Primary Science Review*, 5: 6–7.

de Bóo, M. (1988a) Supporting science: reflections of an advisory teacher. *Education 3–13*, 16 (3): 12–16.

de Bóo, M. (1988b) Recording work in science: using words. *Primary Science Review*, 7: 12–14.

de Bóo, M. (1989) The science background of primary teachers. *School Science Review*, 70 (252): 125–7.

de Bóo, M. (1993a) Level 3-ness! – does it exist? *Primary Science Review*, 29: 6–10.

de Bóo, M. (1993b) Classification skills in the early years. Unpublished paper presented at the Annual Meeting of the Association for Science, Loughborough University of Technology.

de Bóo, M. (1996) Teaching and learning in 4 acts. *Primary Science Review*, 43: 6.

DeLoache, J.S. and Brown, A.L. (1987) The early emergence of planning skills in children, in J.S. Bruner and H. Haste (eds) *Making Sense: The Child's Construction of the World*. London: Methuen.

DES (1984) *Science at Age 11: Assessment of Performance Unit (APU) Report No. 3*. London: HMSO.

Department of Education/Welsh Office (DfE/WO) (1995) *Science in the National Curriculum (1995)*. London: HMSO.

Doise, W. and Mugny, G. (1984) *The Social Development of the Intellect*. Oxford: Pergamon Press.

Donaldson M. (1978) *Children's Minds*. London: Fontana.

Driver, R. (1983) *The Pupil as Scientist*. Milton Keynes: Open University Press.

Driver, R., Guesne, E. and Tiberghiven, A. (1985) *Children's Ideas in Science*. Milton Keynes: Open University Press.

Elstgeest, J. (1985) The right question at the right time, in W. Harlen (ed.) *Primary Science: Taking the Plunge*. London: Heinemann.

Feasey, R. and Thompson, L. (1992) *Effective Questioning in Science* (self-published). Durham: School of Education, University of Durham.

Feynman, R.P. (1986) *Surely You're Joking, Mr Feynman?* London: Unwin Paperbacks.

Fisher, R. (ed.) (1987) *Problem Solving in Primary Schools*. Hemel Hempstead: Simon & Schuster.

Fisher, R. (1990) *Teaching Children to Think*. London: Blackwell.

Frost, R. (1993) *The IT in Primary Science Book*. Hatfield: ASE.

Furth, H.G. (1969) *Piaget and Knowledge: Theoretical Foundations*. Englewood Cliffs, NJ: Prentice Hall.

Galton, M.J., Simon, B. and Croll, P. (1980) *Inside the Primary Classroom*. London: Routledge & Kegan Paul.

Gibson, J. (1998) Any questions, any answers. *Primary Science Review*, 51: 20–1.

Ginsberg, H.P. and Opper, S. (1988) *Piaget's Theory of Intellectual Development* (3rd Edition). New Jersey: Prentice Hall.

Glaser, R. (1984) Education and thinking: the role of knowledge. *American Psychologist*, 39: 93–104.

Glauert, E. (1996) *Tracking Significant Achievement in Science*. London: Hodder & Stoughton.

Gleich, J. (1988) *Chaos: Making a New Science*. London: Heinemann.

Goldsworthy, A. (1989) Observation under observation. *Primary Science Review* 9: 24–6.

Goldsworthy, A. and Feasey, R. (1994) *Making Sense of Primary Investigations*. Hatfield: ASE.

Hadow Report on Primary Education (1931) London: Board of Education, England and Wales.

Harding, J. (1983) *Switched Off: The Science of Education of Girls.* York: Longman, for Schools Council.

Harlen, W. (ed.) (1985) *Primary Science: Taking the Plunge.* London: Heinemann.

Harlen, W. (1996) *The Teaching of Science in Primary Schools,* 2nd edn. London: David Fulton.

Harlen, W. (1997) Teachers' subject knowledge and the teaching of science at primary level. *Science Teacher Education,* 19: 6–7.

Harlen, W. and Symington, D. (1985) Helping children to observe, in W. Harlen (ed.) *Primary Science: Taking the Plunge.* London: Heinemann.

Hawking, S.W. (1988) *A Brief History of Time.* London: Bantam Press.

Hodgson-Burnett, F. (1911) *The Secret Garden.* London: Heinemann.

Hohmann, M., Banet, B. and Weikart, D.P. (1979) *Young Children in Action.* Ypsilanti, MI: High Scope Press.

Holt, J. (1968) *How Children Fail.* Harmondsworth: Penguin.

Holzwarth, W. and Erlbruch, W. (1989) *The Story of the Little Mole Who Knew it Was None of His Business* (English translation). St. Albans: David Bennett Books.

Isaacs, S. (1936) *Intellectual Growth in Young Children.* London: Routledge.

Jabin, Z. and Smith, R. (1994) Using analogies of electric flow in circuits to improve understanding. *Primary Science Review,* 35: 23–6.

Jelly, S. (1985) Helping children raise questions – and answering them, in W. Harlen (ed.) *Primary Science: Taking the Plunge.* London: Heinemann.

Johnsey, R. (1986) *Problem Solving in School Science.* London: MacDonald Education.

Johnson-Laird, P.N. (1983) *Mental Models.* Cambridge: Cambridge University Press.

Johnston, J. (1996) *Early Explorations in Science.* Buckingham: Open University Press.

Kahney, H. (1986) *Problem Solving: A Cognitive Approach.* Milton Keynes: Open University Press.

Karmiloff-Smith, A. (1984) Children's problem solving, in M. Lamb, A. Brown and B. Ragodd (eds) *Advances in Developmental Psychology,* vol. 3, pp. 39–90. Hillsdale, NJ: Erlbaum.

Keogh, B. and Naylor, S. (1997) *Starting Points for Science.* Sandbach, Cheshire: Millgate House.

Kimbell, R., Stables, K., Wheeler, T., Wozniak, A.V. and Kelly, A.V. (1991) *The Assessment of Performance in Design and Technology.* London: HMSO.

Knowles, K. (1993) Learning to teach primary science: a student's view. *Primary Science Review,* 28: 15.

Kuhn, T.S. (1962) *The Structure of Scientific Revolutions.* Chicago: Chicago University Press.

Light, P. and Gilmour, A. (1983) Conservation or conversation? Contextual facilitation of inappropriate conservation judgements. *Journal of Experimental Child Psychology*, 36: 356–63.

Lipman, M. (1974) *Harry Stottlmeier's Discovery*. Upper Montclair, NJ: Institute for the Advancement of Philosophy for Children.

McKee, D. (1980) *Elmer*. London: Red Fox.

McPeck, J. (1981) *Critical Thinking and Education*. New York: St Martin's Press.

Markman, E. and Hutchinson, J. (1984) Children's sensitivity to constraints on word meaning: taxonomic versus thematic relations. *Cognitive Psychology*, 16: 1–27.

Meadows, S. (ed.) (1983) *Developing Thinking: Approaches to Children's Cognitive Development*. London: Methuen.

Menmuir, J. and Adams, K. (1997) Young Children's Inquiry Learning in Mathematics. *TACTYC*, 17 (2): 34–9.

Merry, R. (1998) *Successful Children, Successful Teaching*. Buckingham: Open University Press.

Mischel, T. (ed.) (1971) *Cognitive Development and Epistemology*. New York: Academic Press.

Mitchell, R.P. and Binch, C. (1992) *Hue Boy*. London: Victor Gollancz.

Moffat, J. (1968) *Teaching the Universe of Discourse*. Boston, MA: Houghton-Mifflin.

My First Incredible Dictionary (1994) London: Sherston and Dorling Kindersley Software.

Norris, S.P. (ed.) (1992) *The Generalizability of Critical Thinking*. New York: Teachers' College Press.

Nuthall, G. and Church, J. (1973) Experimental studies of teaching behaviour, in G. Chanan (ed.) *Towards a Science of Science Teaching*. Slough: NFER.

Our Facts (1987) MEP/MESU (Anita Straker). Newman College, Birmingham.

Parker, C. (1991) Geography and IT? *Microscope*, 32: 20–3.

Parkin, R. (1991) Fair play: children's mathematical experiences in the infant classroom, in N. Browne (ed.) *Science and Technology in the Early Years*. Buckingham: Open University Press.

Patefield, J., Jungnitz, S. and Lakin, S. (1993) *Essential Science*. Glasgow: Nelson Blackie.

Paul Hamlyn Foundation (1993) *National Commission on Education Report, 'Learning to Succeed'*. London: Heinemann.

Peacock, A. (ed.) (1991) *Science in Primary Schools: The Multicultural Dimension*. London: Routledge.

Piaget, J. (1929) The child's conception of the world, in H.P. Ginsberg and S. Opper (1988, 3rd edn.) *Piaget's Theory of Intellectual Development*. Englewood Cliffs, NJ: Prentice Hall.

Piaget, J. (1959) *The Language and Thought of the Child*. London: Routledge.

Piaget, J. (1974) *Understanding Causality*. New York: W.W. Norton & Co.

Piaget, J. (1978a) *Success and Understanding*. London: Routledge & Kegan Paul.

Piaget, J. (1978b) *The Development of Thought: Equilibration of Cognitive Structures*. London: Blackwell.

Piaget, J. and Inhelder, B. (1958) *The Growth of Logical Thinking from Childhood to Adolescence* (translated by A. Parsons and S. Seagrin). New York: Basic Books.

Platten, A. (1993) Standardized sheets to encourage children's investigations. *Primary Science Review*, 27: 10–12.

Popper, K. (1988) Science: conjectures and refutations, in E.D. Klemke, (ed.) *Introductory Reading in the Philosophy of Science*. New York: Prometheus Books.

Prestt, B. (ed.) (1980) *Language in Science*. Hatfield: ASE.

Primary SPACE Research Reports (1990 and subsequent years). Liverpool, CRIPSAT (Centre for Research in Primary Science and Technology), Liverpool University Press.

Raper, G. and Stringer, J. (1987) *Encouraging Primary Science*. London: Cassell.

Redfield, D.L. and Rousseau, E.W. (1981) A meta-analysis of experimental research on teacher questioning behaviour. *Review of Educational Research*, 51: 237–45.

Reilly, M. (ed.) (1974) *Play as Exploratory Learning*. Beverley Hills, CA: Sage Publications.

Richardson, J. (1988) *Tall Inside*. London: Methuen.

Ritchie, R. (1995) *Primary Design and Technology: A Process for Learning*. London: David Fulton.

Robinson, E. (1983) Metacognitive development, in S. Meadows (ed.) *Developing Thinking: Approaches to Children's Cognitive Development*. London: Methuen.

Ross, C. and Browne, N. (1993) *Girls as Constructors in the Early Years*. Stoke-on-Trent: Trentham Books.

Ross, K. and Sutton, C. (1982) Concept profiles and the cultural contexts. *European Journal of Science Education*, 4: 311–23.

Russell, T. (1993) An alternative conception: representing representations, in P. Black and A. Lucas (eds) *Children's Informal Ideas in Science*. London: Routledge.

SCAA (1994) *Evaluation of the Implementation of the National Curriculum for Science, Key Stages 1, 2 and 3*. London: HMSO.

SCAA (1995) *Exemplification of Standards: Science*. London: HMSO.

Scottish Office (1993) *Environmental Studies: Science*. Edinburgh: SOED.

Searle, J. (1969) *Speech Acts*. London: Cambridge University Press.

Siegel, H. (1988) *Educating Reason: Rationality, Critical Thinking and Education*. New York: Routledge.

Siraj-Blatchford, J. (1995) Early years design and technology education, *OMEP, Update Number 74*: Spring 1995.

Sneddon, R. (1993) *What is a Fish?* London: Belitha Press.

Stables, K., Kendall, S. and Parker, S. *1991 Key Stage 1 Technology Guidance for INSET Providers*. London: Technology Education Research Unit.

Sutton, C. (1992) *Words, Science and Learning*. Buckingham: Open University Press.

Swift, J.N. and Gooding, C.T. (1983) Interaction of wait time, feedback and questioning instruction in middle school science teaching. *Journal of Research in Science Teaching*, 20: 721–30.

Sylva, K. and Lunt, I. (1982) *Child Development: A First Course*. London: Grant McIntyre.

Symington, D. (1978) Primary school pupils' ability to see investigable scientific problems in everyday phenomena: the teacher's role. *Research in Science Education*, 8: 167–74.

The Lost Frog (1990) MEP/MESU (Anita Straker). Newman College, Birmingham.

The Ultimate Human Body (1994) London: Dorling Kindersley Educational Software.

The Way Things Work (1994) London: Dorling Kindersley Educational Software.

Tizard, B. and Hughes, M. (1984) *Young Children Learning: Talking and Thinking at Home and at School*. London: Fontana.

Tomlinson, J. (1991) *The Cat Who Wanted to Go Home*. London: Reed International Books Ltd.

Torrance, E.P. (1977) *What Research Says to the Teacher: Creativity in the Classroom*. Washington: National Education Association.

Tough, J. (1973) *Focus on Meaning*. London: Allen & Unwin.

Tough, J. (1977) *The Development of Meaning*. London: Allen & Unwin.

Townend, C., Petrenas, A. and Street, L. (1991) Supporting language learning through doing science, in A. Peacock (ed.) *Science in Primary Schools: The Multicultural Dimension*. London: Routledge.

Tuma, D.T. and Reif, F. (1980) *Problem Solving and Education: Issues in Teaching and Research*. Hillsdale, NJ: Erlbaum.

UNESCO (1993) *International Forum on Scientific and Technological Literacy for All. Final Report*. Paris: UNESCO.

Vygotsky, L. (1986) *Thought and Language*. Cambridge, MA: MIT Press.

Wenham, M. (1995) *Understanding Primary Science Ideas, Concepts and Explanations*. London: Paul Chapman.

Westbury, I. (1972) Conventional classrooms, 'open' classrooms and the technology of teaching. *Journal of Curriculum Studies*, 5: 2.

Wood, D. (1988) *How Children Think and Learn*. Oxford: Blackwell.

Wood, D., Bruner, J. and Ross, G. (1976) The role of tutoring in problem solving. *Journal of Child Psychology and Psychiatry*, 17 (2): 89–100.

Wood, L. (1997) Play: future directions. *TACTYC*, 17 (2): 28–33.

Yeoman, J. and Blake, Q. (1994) *The Do-It-Yourself House that Jack Built*. London: Puffin.

Index